A Discovery Learning Programme for Primary Geography

Unlocking Geography 5th Class

First published in 2013 by: Folens Publishers,

Hibernian Industrial Estate, Greenhills Road,

Tallaght, Dublin 24.

Educational Consultants: Simon and Rozz Lewis

Acknowledgements: Alamy, Getty Images, Glow Images, iStockphoto, Sciencephoto, Shutterstock and Thinkstock.

ISBN: 978-1-78090-096-4

© 2013 Folens Publishers

The paper used in this book is sourced from managed forests.

Folens books are protected by international copyright laws. All rights reserved.
The copyright of all materials in this book, except where otherwise stated, remains the property of Folens Publishers. No part of this publication may be reproduced, stored in a retrieval system or transmitted in any form or by any means (stencilling, photocopying, etc.) for whatever purpose, even purely educational, without the prior written permission of the publisher. The publisher reserves the right to change, without notice, at any time the specification of this product. The publisher has made every effort to contact copyright holders but if any have been overlooked we will be pleased to make any necessary arrangements. To the best of the publisher's knowledge, information in this book was correct at the time of going to press.
No responsibility can be accepted for any errors.

Contents

Introduction 5

Chapter 1   Earth and Sun... 12

Chapter 2   The Natural Environment and Us 18

Chapter 3   Field Trip: Weather 24

Chapter 4   Survival of the Salmon 32

Chapter 5   Rocks 40

Chapter 6   Working in Ireland 48

Chapter 7   Natural Features: Energy and Tourism 56

Chapter 8   The Counties of Ireland 62

Chapter 9   Land and Water in Ireland 70

Chapter 10   Travelling and Commuting to Work 78

Chapter 11   Fishing in Ireland 86

Chapter 12   Weather and Climate 94

Chapter 13   Latvia 102

Glossary 110

Maps 113

Introduction

'**Unlocking Geography**' is a complete geography programme for teachers, parents and pupils. It covers the geography curriculum from 3rd to 6th Class and has been developed by primary school teachers. For each class the textbook, teacher's manual and exclusive digital resources are integrated to create a unique learning experience.

The programme has three main objectives:

1. The creation of a seamless and blended approach to the teaching and learning of geography using active learning, collaborative learning and the incorporation of digital resources that have been specifically designed to complement the programme.

2. The development of key components of the geography curriculum: human environments; natural environments; environmental awareness and care.

3. The establishment of a geography series that focuses on the key skills of a geographer:
   - questioning
   - observing
   - predicting
   - investigating and experimenting
   - estimating and measuring
   - analysing
   - recording and communicating
   - a sense of place and space
   - maps, globes and graphical skills
   - geographical investigation skills

Chapter Opener

Each chapter opens with a motivating 'hook'. This can be used as an introduction to the topic and lesson. Pupils are drawn into each new topic using a range of stimuli that set the tone for the lesson to follow.

Think and Discuss
Pupils are asked to think about and discuss what they can see in the chapter; in doing so, previous related knowledge is recalled. This provides an opportunity for the development of oral language skills as well as focusing on geographical skills.

What Will I Learn?
The curriculum objectives are vitally important for the teacher to plan their lesson. From the curriculum objectives, the pupils are given clear, easy-to-follow learning objectives at the start of every chapter.

Key Vocabulary
Any new vocabulary that is being introduced is presented here. There are many activities that can stem from this. The teacher may need to ensure that all key vocabulary is understood before the lesson development. The key vocabulary is also highlighted throughout each chapter and explained in the glossary section.

The Key to Literacy
The Key to Literacy is an effective tool used to integrate the English curriculum into the geography curriculum in a meaningful way that supports the aims of the geography curriculum.

Checkpoint
These activities are designed to help facilitate the recall of any geographical knowledge that has been learned. Checkpoints link in with the chapter's learning outcomes and are a useful revision tool.

Research and Write It/Over to You/Design and Draw
Each of these sections provide ideas for further extension work in the particular area of geographical discovery. This may involve research using the internet, books or real-life research.

Geographical Investigation Skills/Map Skills
These activities require the use of an atlas, encyclopaedia or the internet in order to investigate the local environment. They also provide a chance to apply and develop map skills.

Lesson Wrap-Up/Visual Summary

This component of the chapter provides a quick revision of the chapter's main ideas and themes. This also signals the final part of the lesson to the teacher.

Review

The Review focuses on recalling information and vocabulary, critical thinking and developing the skills of a geographer.

What Did I Learn? – Self-Assessment

This section provides an important opportunity to reflect upon the lesson. The following questions are asked at the end of every chapter:

- What have I learned in this chapter?
- What else would I like to know?
- Where can I find this information?

Questions can be linked back to learning outcomes and also enable the teacher to assess information and skills that have been learned, provoking further research into areas the pupils are interested in.

Glossary

This is a useful aid as all the words in the Key Vocabulary section are fully explained here in simple, clear and concise language.

Chapters – Strands – Strand Units

Chapter	Title	Strand Unit
01	Earth and Sun	Natural environments
02	The Natural Environment and Us	Natural environments
03	Field Trip: Weather	Natural environments
04	Survival of the Salmon	Environmental awareness and care
05	Rocks	Natural environments
06	Working in Ireland	Human environments
07	Natural Features: Energy and Tourism	Human environments / Natural environments
08	The Counties of Ireland	Human environments
09	Land and Water in Ireland	Natural environments
10	Travelling and Commuting to Work	Human environments
11	Fishing in Ireland	Human environments
12	Weather and Climate	Natural environments
13	Latvia	Human environments

Unlocking Geography • 5th Class

- Planet Earth in space — 12
- The local natural environment — 18
- Weather, climate and atmosphere — 24
- Caring for the environment — 32
- Rocks and soils — 40
- People living and working in the local area / People living and working in a contrasting part of Ireland — 48
- People living and working in a contrasting part of Ireland / The local natural environment — 56
- County, regional and national centres — 62
- Land, rivers and seas of Ireland — 70
- People living and working in the local area / People living and working in a contrasting part of Ireland — 78
- People living and working in the local area / People living and working in a contrasting part of Ireland — 86
- Weather, climate and atmosphere — 94
- People and other lands — 102

Unlocking Geography • 5th Class

Linkage and Integration

- 01 Earth and Sun
- 02 The Natural Environment and Us
- 03 Field Trip: Weather
- 04 Survival of the Salmon
- 05 Rocks
- 06 Working in Ireland
- 07 Natural Features: Energy and Tourism
- 08 The Counties of Ireland
- 09 Land and Water in Ireland
- 10 Travelling and Commuting to Work
- 11 Fishing in Ireland
- 12 Weather and Climate
- 13 Latvia

Page	Subject links
12	**History** – examine how sundials were used to tell time by the Romans and ancient Egyptians **Visual arts** – discuss depictions of sunrise and sunset in artistic works
18	**Maths** – use the trundle wheel, metre sticks and measuring tapes to measure distances **Gaeilge** – caitheamh aimsire
24	**History** – examine people related to weather, e.g. Anders Celsius and Sir Francis Beaufort **Music** – compose a musical piece to sound like a weather event, e.g. a thunder storm
32	**English** – read Fionn Mac Cumhaill and the Salmon of Knowledge in class, discuss significance of salmon in Irish history **History** – create a timeline of events from the story of Fionn Mac Cumhaill and the Salmon of Knowledge
40	**History** – explore the Stone Age and how people have used rocks since **English** – read and discuss non-fiction pieces on earthquakes and volcanoes
48	**History** – explore Irish emigration, especially after the Great Famine **Science** – examine the role of science in high-tech industries
56	**Science** – recognise that burning fossil fuels creates heat, explore types of fuels **History** – explore how the local area has changed using old photographs and maps
62	**History** – examine historical settlements, churches and monasteries in Irish counties **Gaeilge** – explore the differences between the Irish and English versions of county names and their meanings
70	**English** – write an imaginative piece on living on an island during a storm **Maths** – compare lengths of Irish rivers
78	**Maths** – examine a variety of timetables and work out journey times, costs, frequency, etc. **Science** – examine how technological developments have helped transport
86	**English** – write a blog for a fisherman, describing the fish he catches, weather conditions, his routine, etc. **Drama** – childen can take turns interviewing one another for the job advertised in the lesson
94	**Maths** – examine positive and negative numbers in the context of temperatures **Gaeilge** – examine vocabulary related to the weather
102	**Visual arts** – design packaging for Laima chocolate **SPHE** – explore thoughts and feelings around how people from other cultures are treated in Ireland

Unlocking Geography • 5th Class

1 Earth and Sun

What Will I Learn?

- To explain what the sun is.
- To make a sundial and use the sun's shadows to tell the time.
- To understand the sun's impact on days and seasons.
- To describe how the sun affects plants and animals.

Blog

Hi, I'm Fergal. I'm a farmer from Newtown in County Louth. I took over the family business about ten years ago. It's a mixed farm. The farm produces cattle, sheep, poultry, vegetables and grain.

I have spent my whole life working outdoors. I can tell what time of year it is just by looking at where the sun is in the sky and how bright it is. The farming year starts in autumn, when the days are growing shorter and the sun is getting lower in the sky. With winter on its way, the light from the sun is less intense. The days are colder and the grass stops growing. Very early on winter mornings, when I go down to feed the chickens it is still dark. After breakfast, I plough the fields. I have to work fast as the days are short. My tractor casts long shadows across the fields.

In spring it can be exciting to feel the sun growing stronger, and to see it rising higher in the sky each day as the days begin to lengthen. I plant many of my crops at this time of year. In summer, when the sun is highest in the sky, the crops grow fast. July and August are harvest time. It's a busy time but luckily the days are long. Some evenings I'm still out in the fields at 9 p.m. I wear sunglasses to protect my eyes and rub on sunscreen to stop myself from becoming sun burnt. Before you know it, it's autumn again and another year has gone by.

Think and Discuss

1. Why do you think most crops are planted in spring?

2. How, do you think, do the shorter days in winter affect the animals on a farm? How does the summer heat affect them?

3. During which months of the year is it dark when you get up for school?

4. What is your favourite season? What is the sunlight like at that time of year?

5. At what time of year do you have to be careful about the effect of strong sunlight on your eyes and skin?

KEY VOCABULARY

orbits   solar system   axis
sunburn   sunstroke   sundial
rotation   hemisphere

Unlocking Geography • 5th Class   13

The Sun

The sun, like all stars, is made up of burning hot gasses. It is 150 million km away from the Earth, yet it is our closest star. It is also the biggest star in the solar system, so big, that our planet could fit into it one million times! The sun heats and lights our world. At its core, it is 15 million degrees Celsius. Without the sun, there would be no life on Earth. In fact, it would be so cold, that our planet would be completely frozen.

The sun is at the centre of our solar system. The Earth moves, or orbits, around it. It takes the Earth 365 days (a full year) to orbit the sun, and this is what gives us seasons. The Earth also rotates on its own axis every 24 hours, giving us night and day. The sun rises in the east and sets in the west because the Earth spins towards the east.

The sun is essential to all life on Earth. It provides energy for every plant and animal and it is the first part of the food chain. The energy from the sun enables plants to grow, using photosynthesis. Plants use the sun's light energy to make food. Herbivore animals, like rabbits, eat plants such as grass. Carnivore animals, like snakes, eat rabbits and they, in turn, are eaten by larger animals such as owls. Green plants use energy from the sun to change water, carbon dioxide and minerals into the oxygen that we all breathe. Without photosynthesis, most of the living things on Earth would disappear and the Earth's atmosphere would run out of oxygen. Without the sun, photosynthesis could not happen.

Did You Know?
Ultra-violet (UV) rays from the sun can cause skin and eye damage, sunburn, sunstroke, skin cancer and allergic reaction. When we are exposed to sunlight on hot days, we should wear sun protection like creams, sprays, sunglasses and protective clothing.

Not only does the sun help trees, plants, flowers and animals to grow, but people depend on it for energy in the form of vitamin D. Farmers like Fergal get a lot of help from the sun when they are growing crops in summertime.

Think About It

1. At what time of the day is the sun most likely to burn you? Why do you think this is?
2. Do people ever need to protect themselves from the sun on a cloudy day? Why?

CHECKPOINT

1. What is the sun?
2. How does the sun affect the seasons?
3. What is the sun's role in photosynthesis?
4. List four dangers of the sun.
5. List some ways people can stay safe in the sun.

Telling the Time

Ancient civilisations noticed that the sun cast shadows of different lengths at specific times of the day. They used a special kind of clock called a sundial to tell the time. Follow the instructions below to make your own sundial.

Let's Investigate

What You Need:
- Stick or pole that can be pushed into the ground
- Large piece of paper – at least A3
- Pencil
- Ruler
- Watch

Important! Never look directly at the sun.

What to Do:
1. Place your piece of paper down on a flat piece of ground.
2. Stick the pole through the centre of the page into the ground.
3. Using the ruler and pencil, draw a line following the shadow. Make sure to keep note of the lengths, as this will tell you how high the sun is.
4. Check your watch. What time is it? Record the time at the end of the line.
5. Mark the position of the shadow cast by the stick every hour. Write the time beside this mark.
6. After doing this a few times, you should be able to estimate where the shadow will be at the next hour.

Over to You
1. How does the position of the shadow change throughout the day?
2. At what time is the sun highest in the sky?

Did You Know?
It takes the Earth 24 hours to make a single turn. As the Earth rotates, the part that is facing the sun experiences daylight.

Seasons

As we have discovered, it takes the Earth one full day (24 hours) to make a complete turn on its axis, and this is how we experience night and day. It takes the Earth one full year (365 days) to orbit or travel all the way around the sun. The Earth is tilted on its axis and has an imaginary line of latitude around its centre, known as the equator. The part of the Earth that is 'above' or north of the equator is called the northern hemisphere, while the part of the Earth that is 'below' or south of the equator is called the southern hemisphere.

Look at Ireland on a globe. You will see that our country is located in the northern hemisphere. We have our summer months during May, June and July. This is because at that time of year, the northern hemisphere is tilted towards the sun. Countries like Australia and New Zealand have their winter during this time because they are in the southern hemisphere. While we are tilting towards the sun, they are tilting away from it. Experiment with a globe and a lamp to see how the sun shines on the orbiting Earth.

Did You Know?
In Australia, summer months are December, January and February. So the Australian Christmas happens in summertime!

The Key to Literacy
Imagine you are spending Christmas away from home in Australia. Write a letter to your friend describing what this Christmas is like and how it compares to Christmas at home. Use the Internet to find out some interesting things about Christmas in Australia.

Let's Investigate

What You Need:
- Globe
- Lamp/torch
- Piece of white card with a hole in it

What to Do:

1. Put the globe on a table and stand the lamp about a metre away. Tilt the globe so that the North Pole is facing away from the lamp. If you imagine that the lamp is the sun, this is the position the Earth is in during the winter.

2. Hold the sheet of card between the globe and the lamp so that a narrow beam of light shines onto the surface of the globe.

3. Examine the light on the globe. Identify the area where it is brightest.

4. Next, tilt the globe so that the North Pole is leaning towards the lamp. Imagine the lamp is the sun. This is the position the Earth is in during summer time in Ireland.

Visual Summary

The sun is a star made up of burning hot gases. It is the largest object in the Solar System and the closest star to Earth.

It takes the Earth 24 hours to make a single turn. The part of the Earth facing the sun during its **rotation** experiences daylight.

It takes the Earth 365 days to orbit the sun. When it is summer in the northern hemisphere, it is winter in the southern hemisphere.

What Did I Learn?

What have I learned in this chapter?

What else would I like to know?

Where can I find this information?

Review

1. **Recall**
   What temperature is the sun at its core?

2. **Vocabulary**
   Sundial, sunscreen and sunshine are all words that feature the word 'sun'. How many other words can you make using the word 'sun'? Make a list.

3. **Critical Thinking**
   Prepare a one-minute talk on sun safety for your classmates. Outline the dangers of the sun, then describe how to protect different parts of the body, such as your head, skin and eyes.

4. **Be a Geographer!**
   Imagine you are a farmer like Fergal, trying to make up a schedule of work to be done on the farm. List the outside jobs that need to be done during daylight hours, and the inside jobs that can be done in the dark during the winter months.

2. The Natural Environment and Us

What Will I Learn?

- How natural features in Ireland and my locality influence the activities people take part in.
- The effect that the natural environment has on the work that people do outdoors.
- How waterways and land drainage are important in the work of a farmer.

Blog

The Burren: A Potholer's Paradise

Hello! My name is Yvonne and I live in Galway. I work in a library in the city.

In my spare time, I enjoy . Potholing is a name for the exploration of caves and cave systems deep underground. Ireland is a brilliant country to do this in, as there are many areas with interesting and challenging caves for potholers to visit. We sometimes have to lower ourselves into the caves using ropes and special equipment. We always wear a hard hat to protect our heads and torches are very important if we want to see what's down there! You wouldn't believe some of the tight spaces we squeeze through in the rock to get from one part of a cave to another. This pastime is definitely not for people who panic in small spaces! It is worth it when we see things like waterfalls, unusual rock formations and glittering minerals.

I am part of a club that explores the caves of the Burren region in County Clare. The limestone rock of the Burren has a wealth of caves. When it rains, the water drains down through the rocks and creates large, fast-flowing underground rivers. It is a side of our natural environment in Ireland that people do not often get to see.

Think and Discuss

1. What would you find interesting about an activity like potholing?
2. What would you dislike about potholing?
3. Limestone can easily be broken down over time by the action of rainwater. How, do you think, has this helped to create the many caves in the Burren?
4. Find out if there are any potholing clubs or caves near you. Do you know whether the caves go very far into the earth?

 KEY VOCABULARY

potholing

abseiling

pastime

drainage system

Unlocking Geography • 5th Class

My Local Area

Every county in Ireland has its own range of natural features. For this reason, counties here may look quite different from one another. The natural features in an area have a big impact on what people there do, both for leisure and work. The grassy countryside of County Kildare has become very well-known for horse riding. Ireland is also a popular destination for outdoor activities. Fishing, abseiling, potholing and sailing could not be done without the natural features around us. Natural features such as mountains and rivers influence how we get from one place to another and where we build our roads and bridges. As we will see, natural features such as rivers and streams have a direct impact on the lives of those who work on the land, such as farmers. It can be surprising the amount of different ways our local natural environment has shaped how we all live our lives.

Think and Discuss

1. Why, do you think, is County Kildare a suitable area for horse riding?
2. Apart from the activities mentioned, what other activities rely on natural features?

Geographical Investigation Skills

Make a list of some of the outdoor activities that people near you enjoy doing in their spare time. How are they making use of their natural environment? Are there parts of Ireland where it is not possible to do these things? Why is that?

Design and Draw

Think of a new way to use a natural feature. It could be a mountain, lake, river, beach or other piece of land. Describe what the activity would be and how the natural feature would be used in carrying out the activity. Draw a picture of the activity and an outline map of the area you would use.

Think About It

Do you think your locality is using its natural features well? Why/Why not?

Blog

Farming and Drainage

Welcome to our farm. This is Terry Calvin here and I'm in charge of Streamview Farm. We are a large operation and grow vegetables which we supply to markets and customers nationwide. We are famous for our cabbages and cauliflowers in particular. We like to keep people informed about news from the farm so we hope you enjoy our current update.

Latest News

3rd February

It's been a wet season here on the farm and because our farm is built near a stream, it often floods. If we want to keep our crops growing, we have to work hard to prevent the stream from flooding our land. If we allowed the stream to flood, our land would be waterlogged for weeks. That would mean that our crops would suffocate in all that water and die. However, a positive aspect of being located near a stream is that the soil is really good for growing crops, because of the nutrients the steam brings to the soil. Our crops grow really well because we have a good ==drainage system==. Our land is built on a slope, which means that any surface water flows down it and out of harm's way. Just in case that is not enough, I also have underground drains, so if too much water gets through the soil, it has somewhere to flow. Still, we are looking forward to summer, when hopefully, the weather will be sunny and dry.

Think and Discuss

1. How does the natural environment around Streamview Farm affect the work that the farmer has to do?
2. Why is it important to have a drainage system on a farm?
3. What are the advantages of farming by a waterway, such as a stream?
4. What are the disadvantages of farming by a waterway, such as a stream?
5. What would you do if you were Terry and there was a severe flood warning?

The Key to Literacy

Imagine you have to sell Terry's farm. Write an advertisement explaining the reasons that someone should buy it.

Drainage at Your School

We are going to investigate whether your school deals with drainage well. It is probably best to do this after it has been raining so you can see the results more clearly. Depending on the size of your school, you might need to divide into groups to investigate different sections of your school. For example: the yard, the entrance to the school, or the school's garden. Before you investigate, make sure you have the required equipment.

Let's Investigate Drainage

What You Need:
- A sheet of white paper (for a map of the school)
- A pencil
- Some coloured crayons or markers
- An eraser
- A ruler, a trundle wheel or a measuring tape for measuring around your school

What to Do:
1. Draw a map of your school. It should show where the school building is and the areas outside that you are going to observe.

2. Create a map 'key' and use symbols to mark water, grass, concrete, and water drains.

3. If your area contains grass and concrete, make sure to use colour or shading to show the difference. Sketch in blue areas where you can see water on the surface. Try to measure the size of the puddles and mark them on your map. You will need a ruler or other measuring tool for this, such as a measuring tape or trundle wheel.

Evaluating the Results
1. Describe the surface water coverage in the area of the school you investigated.
2. Do you think your school has a good drainage system? Why?
3. What could be done to improve the drainage system in your school?

Lesson Wrap-Up

Visual Summary

The natural environment and its features changes from place to place in Ireland. It affects how we work and influences the activities we take part in.

Farmers are very aware of the relationship between their work and the natural environment around them. That is why proper drainage is very important in farming.

We can study the effects of poor drainage in our school or local area.

Review

1. **Recall**
   What type of rock is found in the Burren region of County Clare?

2. **Vocabulary**
   In this lesson we study how drainage systems affect our lives. Name another 'system' in the natural world that affects how we live.

3. **Critical Thinking**
   Identify three jobs that people do your locality that are influenced by the natural features around you. How does the natural environment affect the work that these people do?

4. **Be a Geographer!**
   Design a drainage system for your school that would keep surface water off the playground as much as possible. You can make a sketch of it to share with the class.

What Did I Learn?

What have I learned in this chapter?

What else would I like to know?

Where can I find this information?

Unlocking Geography • 5th Class

3 Field Trip
Weather

What Will I Learn?

- About the work of a **meteorologist**.
- How to measure wind speed and direction, temperature, precipitation, **atmospheric pressure** and cloud cover.
- To record and report the weather.

Blog

Hi there, I'm Jessica and I work as a meteorologist in Met Éireann. I study the weather and give weather forecasts. A **forecast** is a prediction of what the weather will be like in the coming days. We don't just guess what the weather will be like; we use information from our weather stations and computer programmes to help us. Every hour, readings for wind direction and speed, temperatures, atmospheric pressure, cloud amounts and types are taken. All the readings are coded and entered into a computer; then they are sent to me in Glasnevin, where I work. My job is to analyse this data so I can prepare weather maps, which you see on TV and in newspapers.

Today, you'll be going on a field trip to discover weather patterns in your locality. Depending on the time of the year, you might get completely different results. You will be measuring the weather in much the same way as the centres. The following will be measured: wind, temperature, precipitation, air pressure and clouds. These are the items you'll need:

- Pencil and rubber
- Compass
- **Anemometer**
- Wind vane
- **Barometer**
- **Rain gauge**
- **Thermometer**
- Digital camera

Unlocking Geography • 5th Class

Think and Discuss

1. List some ways that we can find out about the weather.
2. Why, do you think, do people need to know about the weather?
3. What is a meteorologist?
4. What needs to be measured in order to analyse and predict the weather?

 KEY VOCABULARY

meteorologist **forecast**
thermometer
anemometer
rain gauge
barometer
atmospheric pressure

Unlocking Geography • 5th Class   25

Measuring Wind

In this section, you are going to learn how wind is measured. Wind is simply air moving from one place to another. Winds are named after the direction they are coming from, so a north wind always comes from the north and usually brings cold weather from the North Pole. Winds sometimes bring hot weather too. In Ireland, these usually come from the tropical regions of Earth.

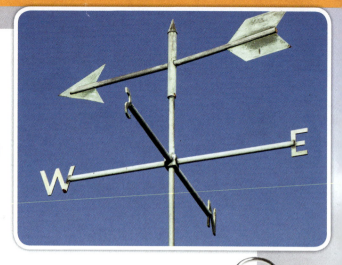

To measure the wind, you'll need a wind vane and compass so you can see the direction that the wind is blowing in.

- First measure the wind direction using the wind vane.
- Place your compass near the wind vane.
- Check which direction the vane is pointing to using the compass.
- Record your result in your field trip log.

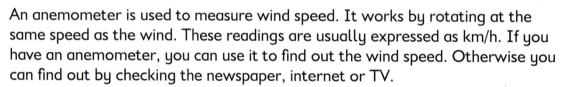

An anemometer is used to measure wind speed. It works by rotating at the same speed as the wind. These readings are usually expressed as km/h. If you have an anemometer, you can use it to find out the wind speed. Otherwise you can find out by checking the newspaper, internet or TV.

When you have found the wind speed you can use the Beaufort Wind Scale to find out the force of the wind. The Beaufort Wind Scale is a scale that goes from 0 to 12, where zero is calm and twelve is a hurricane. Remember to record the wind speed and number on the Beaufort Wind Scale in your field trip log.

Beaufort Number	Wind Type	Wind Speed
0	Calm	0 km/h
1	Light air	1–5 km/h
2	Light breeze	6–11 km/h
3	Gentle breeze	12–19 km/h
4	Moderate breeze	20–28 km/h
5	Fresh breeze	29–38 km/h
6	Strong breeze	39–49 km/h
7	Moderate gale	50–61 km/h
8	Fresh gale	62–74 km/h
9	Strong gale	75–88 km/h
10	Whole gale (or storm)	89–102 km/h
11	Storm (or violent storm)	103–114 km/h
12–17	Hurricane	117 km/h and above

Measuring Temperature

Temperature is measured in degrees Celsius. 0 degrees is called freezing point – and is the point at which ice begins to melt. 100 degrees is called boiling point. A comfortable room temperature is about 20 degrees. There are lots of types of thermometers but the one that is used most often is called a mercury thermometer.

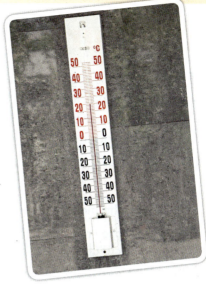

How a Mercury Thermometer Works

A thermometer is a glass tube that is full of a liquid metal called mercury. Mercury expands when it is heated and shrinks when it cools. When the temperature outside the thermometer increases, the mercury inside the glass will then rise. A scale on the outside of the tube shows what degree Celsius the temperature is.

Over to You

Use a thermometer to measure the temperature outside.

1. Place the thermometer in an unsheltered area.
2. Wait for a few minutes and look at the thermometer. Read the temperature on the scale.
3. Record the results in your field trip log.

Graphic Forecast

The weather can be shown in graphics. This chart shows the weather, wind and temperature forecast for five days.

Forecast	Monday	Tuesday	Wednesday	Thursday	Friday
Weather	⛅	🌧️	⛈️	⛅	🌧️
Wind	13 km/h	19 km/h	22 km/h	17 km/h	13 km/h
Temperature	16°C	12°C	18°C	19°C	10°C

Think About It

1. Which days are predicted to be hottest and coldest?
2. On which days is there heavy rain forecast?
3. Write a sentence describing the weather on Thursday.

Looking at Clouds

Believe it or not, clouds can tell us a lot about the weather. A cloud is made from tiny particles of water and ice crystals. Depending on the shape and height of a cloud, we can find out a lot about the type of weather we are having. The only equipment you need for this next experiment is your eyes.

- Choose a position outside and look up at the sky.
- Look at the clouds and describe them.
- Read the chart and look at the photographs to find out the name of the type of cloud you are looking at.
- Record your result in your field trip log.

Description	Type of Cloud	Weather
wispy sheets, layers, blankets	Cirrus, Stratus	windy, maybe stormy drizzle, fog
fluffy, billowy	Cumulus	rain, sunny or showery depending on size

Cumulus

Cirrus

Cloud cover is usually measured in oktas. This is a scale from 0 to 8, where 0 means a clear sky and 8 means that the sky is completely covered by cloud. A half-filled sky would have a measurement of 4.

- Choose a position outside and look up at the sky.
- Give the sky a rating of 0 to 8 based on the oktas scale described above.
- Record your result in your field trip log.

Stratus

The Key to Literacy

Many new words have been introduced in this chapter. Can you remember what they all mean? Do you have any ways to help you remember them?

Lesson Wrap-Up

Visual Summary

Wind can be measured using a number of instruments. A compass and wind vane can tell us the direction wind is blowing while an anemometer tells us the wind speed.

Temperature is usually measured using a mercury thermometer. Precipitation like hail, rain and snow can be measured using a rain gauge. A barometer is used to measure atmospheric pressure.

Clouds are made up of tiny water particles and ice crystals. By looking at the shape and height of a cloud, we can find out a lot about the weather. The main types of cloud are cirrus, stratus and cumulus.

Review

1. **Recall**

   What is precipitation? How is it measured?

2. **Vocabulary**

   What does 'atmospheric pressure' mean? Use the term in a sentence.

3. **Critical Thinking**

   Explain why it is important for some people's work to know about temperature, rainfall, wind direction and wind speed. Use at least three jobs as examples.

4. **Be a Geographer!**

   Create a weather report using the data collected on the field trip. Then use the internet or other sources to help you prepare a forecast for the next three days for your area.

What Did I Learn?

What have I learned in this chapter?

What else would I like to know?

Where can I find this information?

4 Survival of the Salmon

What Will I Learn?

- About the salmon and its life cycle.
- About the threats that impact the future of salmon.
- How Irish laws seek to prevent overfishing of salmon.
- Facts about water pollution.

Think and Discuss

1. What do all the photographs have in common?
2. Write a caption for each of the photographs.
3. Which is your favourite photograph?
4. Which is your least favourite photograph?
5. How do the photographs relate to the fishing industry in Ireland?

KEY VOCABULARY

fishmonger   pollution

reproduce   spawn

upstream   degrade

Unlocking Geography • 5th Class   33

Salmon – A Popular Irish Fish

Blog

Hello! My name is Chris and I work as a fishmonger. My favourite fish that we sell is salmon and I love telling customers all about it. Salmon makes a nutritious and tasty meal. Large amounts of salmon are sold in Ireland every year. Quotas have been introduced to ensure that salmon is not overfished. This ensures the salmons' survival in Ireland for generations to come.

Salmon live in the sea and in fresh water. Our rivers and lakes have to be kept free from any sort of pollution, as a polluted river would not be a good habitat for the salmon.

The salmon is full of goodness and is rich in healthy fish oils, which are good for keeping your brain, skin, hair and nails healthy. I love eating a salmon steak with a simple salad and some brown bread – delicious!

CHECKPOINT

1. Why does Chris say that quotas on salmon fishing have been introduced?
2. Why is salmon a healthy food?

The Key to Literacy

Salmon has an important place in old Irish myths and legends. Read the story of Fionn Mac Cumhaill and the Salmon of Knowledge. It tells the tale of a magic salmon that would make anyone who ate it the wisest person in Ireland. Write out the story in your own words.

Did You Know?

Salmon are anadromous fish – this means they live in the sea but reproduce in fresh water (in a stream or lake). They live in fresh water throughout their early life, spend adult life in salt water, and then return to fresh water to breed.

Think and Discuss

1. Where, in your local area, is salmon sold? Do you know where this salmon is caught? Is salmon more or less expensive to buy than other types of fish?
2. If you were to visit Chris in his shop, what kinds of questions would you ask him?

The Life Cycle of the Salmon

A salmon spends most of its adult life in the sea. When it is fully grown, it enters fresh water to spawn or reproduce. Salmon eggs, also known as ova, hatch in March or April on the gravel of a river bed. The tiny hatched salmon are called alevins. Three to six weeks after they hatch, alevins begin to swim freely and are called fry. After a short time, the fry start to develop stripes and spots for camouflage. They are then known as parr. A parr feeds and grows in freshwater but its body begins to develop and adapt in preparation for life in salt water. In spring, at the start of its third year of life, a parr becomes a smolt and swims downstream towards the ocean. The smolt stays in the ocean for a year, growing in size and weight. In the summer, the adult salmon stops growing and begins the journey back to the stream where it was born, swimming slowly upstream. The salmon fasts for several months before mating and spawning. Often, a salmon is so tired from fasting and travelling that it does not survive to spawn again.

Ova in freshwater river bed

Newly hatched alevin

Fry develop spots and stripes to become parr

Smolt swim downstream toward the ocean

Adult salmon swim upstream toward the river to spawn

Did You Know?
Some people eat the eggs of salmon. It is called 'salmon roe' and can be quite expensive. It is usually served in small amounts, often on a cracker, or as a garnish.

Think and Discuss

1. Why do we refer to salmon reproduction as a 'cycle'?
2. At which stage in the cycle do you think most salmon are caught to be eaten by humans? Why?
3. The salmon's eggs are laid in a nest on the gravel of the river bed. Can you think of any dangers these eggs might face?

Threats to the Salmon

Natural Threats

The survival of the salmon is threatened in many ways. Some threats are natural and include predatory birds and sea mammals like seals and otters. Other threats include diseases caused by bacteria in the water. Where there are farms close to rivers, cattle can sometimes wander into the water. This disturbs the river bed for spawning salmon.

Human Behaviour

Human behaviour also threatens the survival of salmon. When people plant conifer tress too close to rivers, needles can fall in and make the water too acidic. The flow of a river is very important during the salmons' lifecycle. They need lots of water to be able to migrate upstream and downstream. When people take too much water for industry, agriculture and household use, salmon do not have the volume of water they need for migration. Dams built for water or electricity supply, prevent salmon from passing through on the way to their spawning area. Pollution is another big problem, as salmon need clean healthy water that has lots of oxygen.

Fishing Industry

The fishing industry also affects salmon. Overfishing of smaller fish means some of the salmons' food supply is depleted. Salmon are sometimes caught accidentally by fishermen trying to catch other kinds of fish. Groups of salmon smolts are particularly at risk. When adult salmon try to return to the ocean, fishermen prevent them from spawning by catching them in nets and cages.

Tackling Overfishing

Some new laws in Ireland have tried to arrange for fish passes and these have helped the problem of overfishing. There are also Irish laws to limit the amount of nets that can be used in the Irish coastal waters. Net fishing in fresh water is not allowed. Salmon fishing is also restricted to certain times of the year. This means that during certain months, no salmon fishing is allowed. Between 31 October and the end of December, fishermen are not allowed to fish for salmon. This gives the salmon a chance to begin their spawning season. These laws help the amount of salmon in Irish waters to reach a normal, healthy number.

CHECKPOINT

1. Name three natural threats to the survival of salmon.
2. How does human behaviour affect salmon? Give three examples.
3. List two ways in which overfishing affects salmon.
4. Describe one Irish law that helps prevent overfishing of salmon.

Research and Write It

We know that lots of people love to eat salmon, but what do salmon like to eat? Research and write a list of the different types of food salmon eat. Does an adult salmon eat the same things as it did when it is a young parr?

Did You Know?

For every 8,000 eggs that are produced, 4,500 alevin survive, from which 650 fry survive, from which 200 parr survive, from which 50 smolt survive, from which only 2 spawning adults survive! This also shows why we need to help the salmon to survive.

Think and Discuss

1. What can be done to help the salmon survive?
2. Why, do you think, might it be difficult for fishermen to change the way that they fish?

Pollution – The Facts

Pollution can happen everywhere, not just in the water. We know that land pollution can be very harmful to the environment and all of the creatures who live there. When someone dumps rubbish into the sea, or when land rubbish finds its way into the sea, this can cause major problems for sea animals and some fish such as salmon. Many products take a long time to degrade in the water.

Waste and pollution in the water is not only harmful to humans, animals, fish and plants, it looks very unattractive too. Become involved in projects that help the environment in your local area and always make sure to recycle.

Product	Time it takes to degrade
Cardboard	2 weeks
Newspaper	6 weeks
Styrofoam	80 years
Tinfoil	200 years
Plastic bottles	1000 years
Glass	A million years

Think and Discuss

1. How does water pollution affect plants in the sea?
2. How does water pollution affect fish and other marine animals?
3. What does a dirty, polluted river suggest to tourists about the people who live in an area, do you think? Why?

Design and Draw

Design a poster that you could place beside a local waterway (river, stream or sea) to encourage people to think about their actions and to avoid pollution.

Lesson Wrap-Up

Visual Summary

Large amounts of salmon are sold in Ireland every year. Salmon is a nutritious food because it is rich in healthy fish oils which are good for the hair, skin, nails and brain.

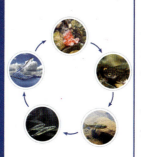
Salmon are anadromous; they spend most of their adult lives in the sea but return to the fresh water rivers where they were born to reproduce.

The survival of the salmon is at risk both from natural threats like bacteria and predatory sea mammals and by human behaviour. Overfishing and pollution are serious threats to salmon.

Review

1. **Recall**
   What is an alevin?

2. **Vocabulary**
   Upstream is a word which has the prefix 'up'. List other words with the same prefix.

3. **Critical Thinking**
   Compare and contrast the life cycle of a salmon with that of a butterfly. How many stages are there? Do the life cycles have anything in common?

4. **Be a Geographer!**
   You are having a picnic by the local river and notice rubbish along the riverbank. Write a letter to the county council with some ideas to deal with the litter problem. Explain how pollution will affect plant and animal life if it continues.

What Did I Learn?

What have I learned in this chapter?

What else would I like to know?

Where can I find this information?

5 Rocks

What Will I Learn?

- About the structure of the Earth using terms such as core, mantle, crust and plates.
- About three different categories of rocks: igneous, sedimentary and metamorphic.
- To name the characteristics of some common rock types and where they may be found in Ireland.
- How to safely investigate rocks in my locality.

Think and Discuss

1. Describe each photograph.
2. Can you see any evidence of rocks that have been changed by humans? Discuss.
3. Why, do you think, may humans have changed some of the rocks?
4. In what other kinds of ways do humans use rocks?

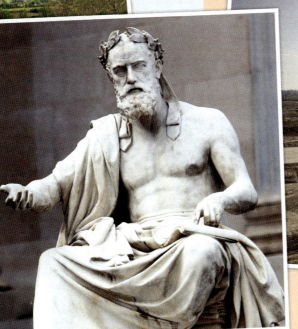

 KEY VOCABULARY

mantle   crust

metamorphic   Pangaea

igneous   core

sedimentary   plates

Unlocking Geography • 5th Class   41

The Earth – Inside Out

If you were to dig a hole in your garden, you would first remove the soft, brown soil near the surface of the ground. After some time, your shovel would hit a much harder area of ground. This is called bedrock.

Geologists who study rocks and the structure of the Earth use enormous drills to take samples from under the Earth's surface. They have been able to dig 12 km into the ground. This may sound quite deep, but keep in mind that the Earth is about 6,400 km from surface to centre.

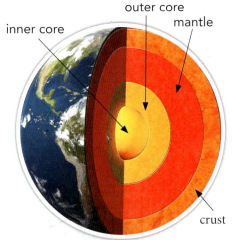

Geologists use various pieces of evidence to help them investigate what lies beneath the Earth's surface. They study waves, created from energy (human or naturally created) and they also study the Earth's magnetic field. These studies help the geologists to understand that the Earth is made of separate layers. These layers are called the crust, the mantle, the outer core and the inner core.

The Crust

The Earth's crust is not a solid shell. It is broken up into huge, thick plates that drift on top of the soft mantle. Earthquakes can happen when two plates rub against one another.

The Mantle

The mantle is the largest section of the Earth's interior. Geologists believe that this layer is made up of scorching hot molten lava. When hot molten lava escapes from the Earth's core it becomes cooler and forms hard rocks, this process is known as volcanism.

The Outer Core

This layer is positioned between the mantle and the inner core. It is made up of iron and is molten liquid in state.

The Inner Core

The inner core is a rock-solid ball of iron and nickel. It is extremely hot.

Earth Changes

Examine a globe or a map of the world in an atlas. Do you notice anything about the size and shape of the continents? Find South America and put your finger on the East Coast. Locate the continent of Africa and put your other finger on the West Coast. You will notice that they look like pieces in a jigsaw that could fit into one other. Try the same with North America and turn it slightly. You will see that it seems to fit into Europe and Asia.

Geologists and scientists started studying these coincidences and found that early fossil records show that the same plants and animals lived along the eastern coast of South America, as did along the western coast of Africa. The same types of plants and animals were found along the coasts of North America and in Europe.

There is strong evidence to suggest that the continents, at one time, were connected to one another. Scientists now believe that there was one huge continent known as Pangaea. It consisted of all the continents on Earth. As the rock plates that the continents sat on moved, Pangaea broke up and began to move apart. This drifting continues to this day and the Earth continues to change.

> **The Key to Literacy**
> Read this section carefully and write down what you think the main idea is. Try to be as clear as you can while using as few words as possible.

CHECKPOINT

1. Name two things geologists study.
2. Draw a picture showing the four layers of the Earth.
3. What happens under the ground to cause earthquakes?
4. What is the Earth's inner core made up of?

Unlocking Geography • 5th Class

Types of Rocks

There are three main types of rocks. They are called igneous, sedimentary and metamorphic rocks. They have their own special characteristics – function, feel and appearance.

Igneous rocks

basalt

granite

All rocks on Earth were originally igneous in nature. Igneous rocks form when liquid magma cools. There are many different types of igneous rock. Granite and basalt are examples of igneous rock.

Sedimentary rocks

sandstone

limestone

Over many millions of years, forces like the wind or water break down the igneous rocks into small pieces that become layered upon each other. Animal and plant remains can also contribute to these layers. Examples of sedimentary rock are sandstone and limestone.

Metamorphic rocks

marble

slate

Metamorphic rocks form when heat and pressure are applied to either igneous rocks or sedimentary rocks. This heat changes their structure significantly. One very common metamorphic rock is marble. Marble and slate are two examples of metamorphic rock.

Map Skills

This map shows the main rocks types in Ireland. Look at it and answer the questions.

1. Name as many types of rocks as you can from looking at this map and key.
2. What is the most common type of rock in your area?
3. What is the most common type of rock in Ireland?
4. What is the least common type of rock in Ireland?

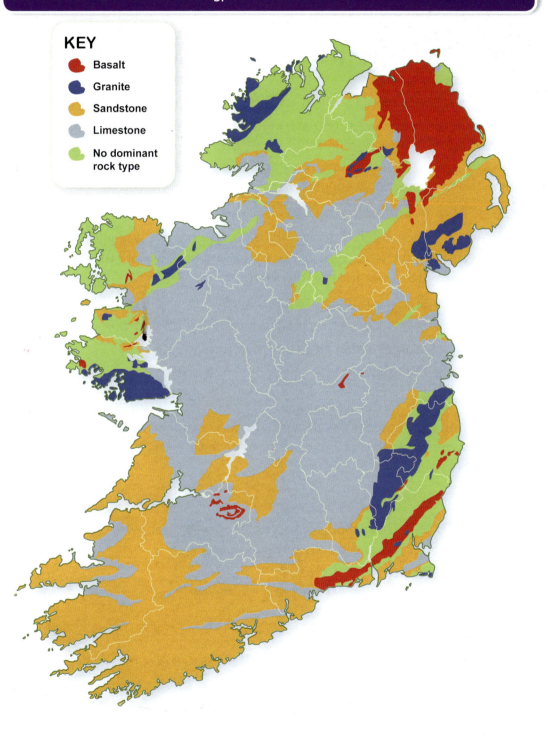

KEY
- Basalt
- Granite
- Sandstone
- Limestone
- No dominant rock type

Unlocking Geography • 5th Class

Local Rocks – An Investigation

This activity involves looking at rocks outside of the classroom, so you will need an adult to go outside with you. You will also need to think about the safety elements to be considered when collecting rocks. Read over these basic rules.

- Collecting rocks should only be carried out under the supervision of an adult.
- Be careful when handling rocks as the rock fragments could have sharp edges.
- Cover rocks with a cloth and wear goggles if you are snapping rocks open later in the classroom.
- Wash your hands after touching any rocks taken from outside.

When you are out and about, you can concentrate on choosing many different types of rocks. You may also find that rocks from your garden are different from those found in your school. Bring them to class to investigate them further. Examine the texture, appearance, colour and hardness of the rocks.

Texture and Appearance

The texture of a rock is how it feels and looks. It can give you information on how it was formed, what type of rock it is, and how people use it. Using a magnifying glass, look out for the following:

- A grainy rough texture (could be sandstone)
- Wavy patterns or stripes (often sedimentary or metamorphic)
- Crystals (sometimes seen in igneous rock like granite)
- Fossils in the rock (could show chalk or limestone)

Colour

Some common rock colours are the grey or tan colour of various types of limestone or the spotted black and white of granite. You might find red sandstone or a black basalt rock.

Hardness

The hardness is something that is taken into consideration when rocks are being used or changed for use in the built environment.

Geographical Investigation Skills

1. Sketch five of the rocks you collected. Try to use colours similar to the real rocks.
2. Write down where each of the five rocks was collected from.
3. Write a brief description of each rock.

Visual Summary

Planet Earth has four layers. They are called the crust, the mantle, the outer core and the inner core.

Scientists believe that the world was once one large continent called Pangaea. Over time, the continents separated and drifted to their current locations.

There are three categories of rock. They are igneous, sedimentary and metamorphic.

What Did I Learn?

What have I learned in this chapter?

What else would I like to know?

Where can I find this information?

Review

1. **Recall**
   What are the three types of rock? How did each type of rock form?

2. **Vocabulary**
   The word metamorphic contains the word morph. Look up the meaning of the word 'morph'. How does this word relate to metamorphic rocks?

3. **Critical Thinking**
   There is a national competition to design a statue for O'Connell Street in Dublin and you wish to enter it. Design and draw your statue. State what rock it should be made from, why it should be made from that rock and what tools might be needed to make it.

4. **Be a Geographer!**
   Think about the importance of rocks. Why would certain people think rocks are important? Write down the importance of rocks for a geologist, a builder and a sculptor.

Unlocking Geography • 5th Class

6 Working in Ireland

What Will I Learn?

- About **migrants** living and working in Ireland.
- About **diversity** in the workplace and why it is important.
- About people who work in Ireland's service industry.
- How to identify services in your local area and show them on a map.

Think and Discuss

1. Describe what you can see in each photograph.
2. What do the photographs all have in common?
3. Does anyone in your class have a family member working in one of these jobs?
4. Which countries do you think the people in these photos come from?
5. Do you think that many jobs in Ireland are done by people from other countries? Which ones?

 KEY VOCABULARY

migrants   dignity
diversity   landlocked
horticulture   discrimination
accessible   economy

Unlocking Geography • 5th Class

Migrant Workers

A migrant worker is a person who comes to live and work in another country. For many years, these workers have helped Ireland's economy to grow. Since the European Union expanded in 2004, many migrants have come to Ireland from countries in Central and Eastern Europe. Today, there is more diversity than ever in the Irish workplace. The 2011 Irish Census listed the top ten migrant nationalities living in Ireland. It revealed that in 2011 Polish people were the largest group of non-Irish nationals and UK migrants were the second biggest group. There are many other nationalities living in Ireland including: Lithuanian, Latvian, Nigerian, Romanian, Indian, Filipino, Chinese, German, French and American. Migrant workers have brought a range of skills and talents to industries like construction, healthcare, horticulture, hospitality and IT. They also contribute to local communities by joining sports clubs, churches, schools and social groups.

The bar chart below shows where migrant workers came from in the years 2006 and 2010.

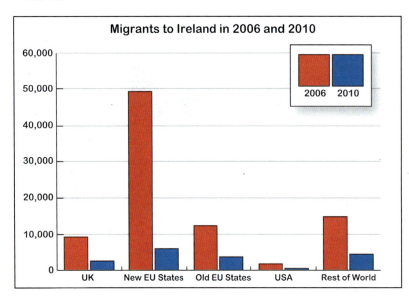

Did You Know?

There are more than 200 million international migrants in the world today. Ireland is also amongst the top ten countries whose nationals live and work overseas.

CHECKPOINT

1. How many migrants came to Ireland from new EU States in 2006?
2. How many migrants came to Ireland from the UK in 2006?
3. Where did most migrants come from in 2010?
4. Where did the least amount of migrants come from in both years?

Think and Discuss

1. Why was there more immigration in 2006 than in 2010?
2. Why, do you think, do migrant workers choose to work in Ireland?

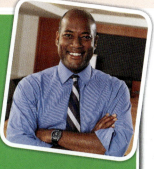

Hi, I'm Adi. I work in advertising. My job is to create slogans and design eye-catching adverts with my team. My wife Cathy is Irish and I came to live here after we got married. I've lived in Athlone for over 20 years so I guess you could say Ireland is my home now. I'll never forget my first home in Africa though. Recently I brought my wife and two kids, John and Matthew, to see Zimbabwe where I grew up.

My name is Kristina and I am from Slovakia. I have been working in Ireland for four years, as the wages are higher here than in Slovakia. I am trying to save enough money so I can buy a house in my home country. For two years I worked as a waitress in Bray until the restaurant closed down. After a long search and lots of interviews, I got a job in a shoe shop, which is great because I love shoes!

I'm Ludwig but most people call me Lud. I'm eleven and I've been living in Ireland since I was eight. I'm in 5th Class and go to school in Shillelagh in County Wicklow. Both my parents work for Kerry Foods, which is just outside the village. My mum is a production manager and my dad is in sales. I'm busy playing basketball, hurling and tennis! I'm on the under 12's hurling team and I only started playing last year! We head back to Riga in Latvia, where I was born, at least twice a year to visit my grandparents and cousins.

Hey there! I'm Xio and I'm in college in Dublin. I've been here for three years now and I'm nearly finished my degree in Agricultural Science. I often visit my family in London, where I was born, especially as flights are so cheap. People complain about the weather here, but it's much the same back home!

Over to You

Locate the four home countries of these migrant workers on a map and answer the questions.

1. Which country is the biggest?
2. Which of the four countries is furthest from Ireland?
3. Both Zimbabwe and Slovakia are landlocked countries. What does this mean, do you think?

The Key to Literacy

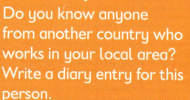

Do you know anyone from another country who works in your local area? Write a diary entry for this person.

Diversity at Work

A diverse workplace is one where staff members are with and without disabilities, of different ages, genders, nationalities, backgrounds and religions. Most people value diversity at work because it allows people to experience new ideas, different approaches to work, and fresh perspectives. It also helps people understand other cultures and ways of life.

Employment Equality Acts were passed under Irish Law in 1998 and 2004. These acts mean that Irish employers have a legal responsibility to make sure that all employees are treated equally.

All employees have a right to dignity and respect in the workplace no matter their age, race, religion, etc.

Sometimes migrant workers face special challenges in the workplace. Problems can occur because of differences in language and culture or if workers are not familiar with Irish Law and do not know their employment rights.

Many companies have taken steps to ensure employees with disabilities have the support and services they need in order to carry out their work. Buildings and bathroom facilities are made wheelchair accessible and special equipment, devices and services are installed for deaf and blind employees.

CHECKPOINT

1. What is a diverse workplace?
2. What do employers in Ireland have to do under the Employment Equality Acts?
3. Name two ways a company can support disabled employees.

Think About It

1. Would you like to work in a diverse workplace? Why?
2. Why is it important to have people from all around the world working and living in Ireland?

Design and Draw

Sometimes people face discrimination at work or in their communities. This can happen where there is a lack of knowledge or understanding. Design a poster that will encourage people to celebrate diversity in Ireland.

Services

A service is something that helps people by providing for their needs and wants. There are many people who offer services in Ireland, both in paid and unpaid employment. People who work in places like medical surgeries, hospitals, banks, chemists, supermarkets, convenience shops, post offices and butchers are all providing a service to customers. National and rural service agencies like local authority county councils and energy suppliers also provide services in Ireland.

Many charities and voluntary organisations offer important services to local communities. Focus Ireland, The Simon Community and Threshold provide services to people who are facing homelessness. Barnardos and the ISPCC provide services for children. The Carers Association send family care workers to the homes of frail older people, terminally ill patients and people with special needs. Cheeverstown offers education, employment and community services to people with learning disabilities.

CHECKPOINT

1. What is a service? Give three examples of people who provide services.
2. What kind of service is provided by the Simon Community?
3. What kind of work is done by the Carers Association?

Think and Discuss

1. Make a list of services available in your local area. Why are these services important?
2. Can you think of a service which is not available in your local area but would be of great benefit?
3. How would you improve one of the services currently provided in your local area?

Services in my Local Area

Now that you have made a list of the local services in your area, show where these services are available using a simple map. Take a look at the sample map on the next page. It shows some of the local services which are available in Killarney, County Kerry. This map has a key or legend with a list of symbols to represent different services.

Map Skills

1. How many doctor surgeries are shown on the map?
2. On which street are the majority of restaurants?
3. How would you identify the town centre on this map?
4. If you lived on Fair Hill road, describe the route you would take to visit your nearest dentist.

Geographical Investigation Skills

Draw a map to show the services that are available in your local area. Include services like those shown in the map above. You may also want to include services in the retail and leisure sectors, e.g. shops, cafes, cinemas, sports areas, as well as any county council offices or local charities. Design symbols for the different services and make sure your map has its own legend or key.

Lesson Wrap-Up

Visual Summary

	A migrant worker is a person who comes to live and work in another country. Many migrants have come to Ireland from Central and Eastern Europe.
	A diverse workplace is one where staff members are with and without disabilities, of different ages, genders, nationalities, backgrounds and religions.
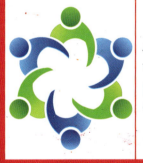	A service is something which helps people by providing for their needs and wants.

Review

1. **Recall**
   What kinds of services are offered by the Cheeverstown charity?

2. **Vocabulary**
   Find out and explain the different meanings of the following words: migrant, immigrant, emigrant and migration.

3. **Critical Thinking**
   What advantages can migrant workers bring Ireland?

4. **Be a Geographer!**
   Visit a public building in your local area, e.g. a library. Look at the parking, entrance and exits, signage and toilet facilities. Write a report to say whether this building is accessible for people with special needs. Consider people in wheelchairs or those with sight or hearing difficulties and suggest some ways that the building could be improved.

What Did I Learn?

What have I learned in this chapter?

What else would I like to know?

Where can I find this information?

7 Natural Features Energy and Tourism

What Will I Learn?
- How natural features can be used to create energy.
- About different sources of energy in Ireland.
- Why tourism is important to Ireland and how natural features can be used to attract tourists.

Blog

Áine, Department of Energy

I work in the government department that deals with energy. We ensure that Ireland has a ==sustainable== supply of energy so that we will always have enough energy to meet our needs. Ireland's natural features provide us with a lot of our energy. For example, we burn peat from our bogs to make electricity, we harness the energy of the River Shannon at the ==hydroelectric power== station in Ardnacrusha, we make use of the winds that blow across our country by creating wind farms, and we are even trying to use the energy of the seas that surround us to create electricity by harnessing ==tidal energy==.

Blog

Barry, Department of Tourism

My department aims to highlight Ireland's natural features to tourists. Ireland has some beautiful and unusual landscapes and features that people love to explore, such as mountains, lakes and rivers. We try to market these fantastic areas to people in Ireland and to people abroad. If tourists come to visit an area of Ireland they spend money there. This benefits everyone: the local businesses such as hotels, shops and restaurants, the transport companies and the government who collect VAT, a tax on products and services purchased by the tourists. Tourism is a really important ==industry== in Ireland.

56 Unlocking Geography • 5th Class

Think and Discuss

1. What do we need energy for?
2. In what ways can we create energy in Ireland?
3. Which companies provide us with energy?
4. Name five tourist destinations in Ireland.
5. If tourists were to visit your county, what could they see and do there?
6. How do we use our natural features for tourism?

 KEY VOCABULARY

sustainable   industry

tidal energy   hydroelectric power

soot   amenities

Unlocking Geography • 5th Class

Natural Features and Energy

We use energy every day. However, we also often take the energy we use for granted. So, where does it come from and will it be with us forever? Read the following stories from people who work in the energy industry to learn more.

Hey! I'm Grace and I'm a tour guide at the Arigna Mining Experience in County Roscommon. Because there are no coal mines anymore, this exhibition shows people what life was like for coalminers until 1990, when the mine closed. Ireland now imports coal from other countries, like Poland. Many people do not use coal for environmental reasons and because it is hard work cleaning soot out of a chimney.

Hi, I'm Stephen and I'm a salesperson for Bord Gáis, Ireland's natural gas suppliers. People don't believe me when I tell them that natural gas is running out. There is only enough gas available to supply Ireland for around 70 more years. Natural gas is the cleanest of the fossil fuels and can be used for almost anything – cooking, heating, barbeques and even tumble-drying.

I'm Sarah and I work for Airtricity, who use the wind to create electricity. I feel very lucky to be part of a team who produce energy in a way that is good for the environment. Wind is a renewable resource, which means there is a continuous source of this energy. I work with a wind farm in County Wexford that produces enough electricity to run 17,000 homes.

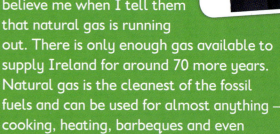

CHECKPOINT

1. Name the four types of energy mentioned in these stories.
2. Which type of energy is the cleanest?
3. What do the following words mean: fossil fuels, soot and turf?

I'm Tom and I live in County Donegal. My mam sometimes asks me to go with her to the bog to help her collect turf. Even though we have electricity, mam says that there is nothing like a proper turf fire. She uses the turf for heating the water and keeping things hot on the range, which also keeps our kitchen lovely and warm on winter days.

Think About It

1. List all the types of energy you can think of. Divide this list into two groups – renewable and non-renewable.
2. Why do you think that non-renewable resources are used more in Ireland today?
3. Do you think this will change in the future?

Welcome to Courtown

Welcome to Courtown, your next holiday destination! Situated in County Wexford, Courtown is one of the most unspoiled seaside resorts on the south-east coast. Why waste time at airports, when Courtown is right on your doorstep? With so much to see and do, you'll be back again and again! Since Courtown Harbour was first built in 1830, it has developed into a very modern resort with many **amenities**. How about a trip along the Ounavarra river, which flows into the bay? You'll go on a journey discovering the history of Courtown from the site of where Courtown House once stood to Ballinatray Bridge, one of the highest old stone-work bridges in the country.

For kids there is ten pin bowling, bumper boats, crazy golf, arcades and games, all within easy reach. Your children will be occupied thoughout your stay.

For a quieter atmosphere, a walk through the Courtown woodland is very enjoyable. With beautiful ash and oak trees over 100 years old, you can choose from several guided walks and bask in their beauty.

Of course, don't forget the beaches. North Wexford is famous for its golden beaches, where you and your family can relax, build sandcastles and paddle in crystal blue waters.

Holiday Ireland Magazine 24

Geographical Investigation Skills

1. Find Courtown on a map. What towns are close by?
2. What natural features are mentioned in the magazine article?
3. How has Courtown used its natural features to attract tourists?

The Key to Literacy

The Local Council in your area are considering building an amusement park on the outskirts of the town. Write them a letter stating why you are for or against the plans and outline how you think the park would affect your town, for better or worse.

8 The Counties of Ireland

What Will I Learn?

- How to recognise counties and **provinces** of Ireland on a map.
- About the major towns and cities in Ireland.
- About my county's **coat of arms**.
- About county **car registration numbers**.

Blog

Hi there! My name is Daniel and I work as a guide on an Irish **tour bus**. In my job, I meet tourists from all over the world: places like America, Italy, Australia and Japan. Tourists enjoy the fact that they can hop on a bus and learn lots of interesting facts about the area they are visiting from an experienced guide. At the moment I divide my time between tours of County Wicklow and County Kerry. My favourite tour to give is the Kerry tour, as I am originally from the town of Tralee, which is the **county town** of County Kerry. I always feel so proud telling tourists about the spectacular scenery in the Ring of Kerry. Sometimes, I even sing songs and recite poems on the tours! I have so many facts in my head to tell tourists, that I never run out of things to say. Next month I start giving tours of County Meath and the Boyne Valley. I am really looking forward to working in this area as I want to learn more about the ancient monuments!

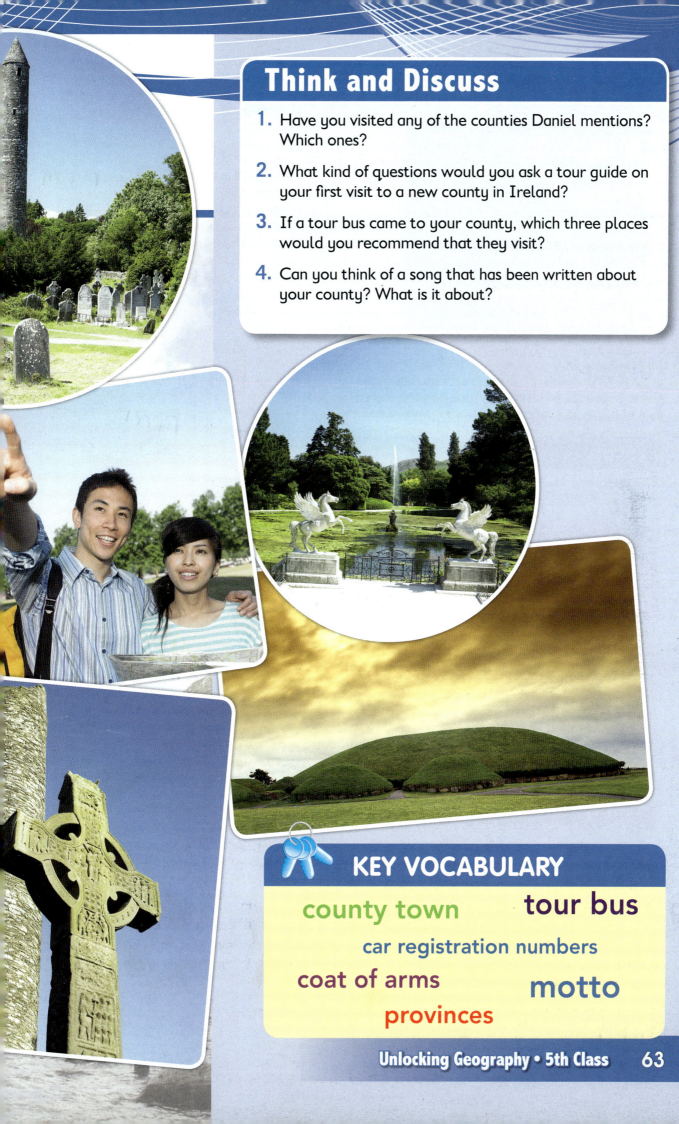

Think and Discuss

1. Have you visited any of the counties Daniel mentions? Which ones?

2. What kind of questions would you ask a tour guide on your first visit to a new county in Ireland?

3. If a tour bus came to your county, which three places would you recommend that they visit?

4. Can you think of a song that has been written about your county? What is it about?

KEY VOCABULARY

county town   tour bus
car registration numbers
coat of arms   motto
provinces

Know Your Counties

Map Skills

Every county on the map of Ireland below has been given a number from 1 to 32. Read the following descriptions for where each county is located. In your copy, write the name of the county and its matching number from the map.

Ulster

The province of **Ulster** is found in the north of Ireland and has nine counties.

County	Location
Donegal	The most northern tip of Ireland
Down	Ireland's most easterly point
Derry	A coastal county, directly east of Donegal
Tyrone	East of Donegal, south of Derry
Fermanagh	South of Tyrone, bordering Donegal
Antrim	East of Derry, north of Down
Armagh	South of Tyrone, bordering Down
Monaghan	Between Armagh and Fermanagh
Cavan	South of Monaghan and Fermanagh

Connaught

The province of **Connaught** is on the west coast of Ireland and has five counties.

County	Location
Sligo	A coastal county, west of Leitrim
Roscommon	South of Sligo, bordering Leitrim
Leitrim	Touching three counties in Ulster
Mayo	West of Roscommon, bordering Sligo
Galway	West of Roscommon, south of Mayo

64 Unlocking Geography • 5th Class

Munster

The province of **Munster** is in the south of Ireland and has six counties.

County	Location
Clare	A coastal county, bordering Galway
Tipperary	Directly east of Clare
Limerick	South of Clare, bordering Tipperary
Cork	Directly south of Limerick, Ireland's largest county
Kerry	In the south west, bordering Cork
Waterford	In the south east, bordering Cork and Tipperary

Leinster

The province of **Leinster** is on the east coast of Ireland and has 12 counties.

County	Location
Kilkenny	North of Waterford and east of Tipperary
Offaly	North of Kilkenny, bordering Galway and Tipperary
Laois	Between Offaly and Kilkenny
Longford	North of Offaly, bordering Roscommon, Leitrim and Cavan
Westmeath	Between Longford and Offaly
Louth	The most northern county in Leinster, on the east coast
Dublin	A coastal county, directly south of Louth
Meath	Bordering Louth and Dublin
Wicklow	A coastal county, directly south of Dublin
Carlow	Small county between Kilkenny and Wicklow
Wexford	A southerly coastal county, bordering Wicklow and Kilkenny
Kildare	Between Meath, Carlow, Laois/Offaly and Wicklow

Think and Discuss

1. Which county do you live in? Which province is it in? Which counties border your county?

2. Some people look at the shapes of the counties and say they look like certain things. For example, the top of County Kerry looks like a person with a hat on. County Carlow has been compared to a carrot and Leitrim to a lamb-chop. What does your county look like? Use your imagination. Choose six counties around Ireland and think of things they might look like.

Towns in Ireland

There are 11 cities in Ireland; Dublin, Cork, Limerick, Waterford, Kilkenny, Derry, Belfast, Galway, Armagh, Newry and Lisburn. Not every county has a city but it does have at least one town.

Geographical Investigation Skills

Find out how many counties have the same name as their main town. For example, Dublin is the main town (and city) of County Dublin and Wicklow is the main town of County Wicklow. Make a graph to show the result.

Blog

I'm Joe and I live in one of County Mayo's main towns, Castlebar. Castlebar is the county town of Mayo, which just means that it is the biggest town in the county. It is not much bigger than our other main towns, Ballina and Westport. Having three big towns in one county has its advantages. For example, if I want to shop for something in Castlebar and it's not there, I have two other towns close by where I can check!

CHECKPOINT

1. What county is Joe from? Name three major towns in his county.
2. What are the major towns in your county? If you have any cities, include those too.
3. What is a county town? Name the county town in your county.

Map Skills

1. Match these towns to their counties: Ennis, Carrick-on-Shannon, Tullamore, Letterkenny, Tralee, Omagh.
2. Using a map, plan a journey starting in Castlebar. You must visit Ballina and Westport then arrive back in Castlebar. Choose the shortest route.
3. Using a map, plan how you would get to Castlebar from where you live.

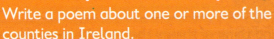

The Key to Literacy
Write a poem about one or more of the counties in Ireland.

My County's Coat of Arms

Every county in Ireland has a coat of arms. This is a design that is usually shaped like a shield and has many features on it. Historically, a coat of arms was the property of a family and every family symbol would have its own design, colour and shape. Usually the coat of arms had a motto, which would indicate a family's achievements. Some countries have a register to make sure that no two families have the same coat of arms.

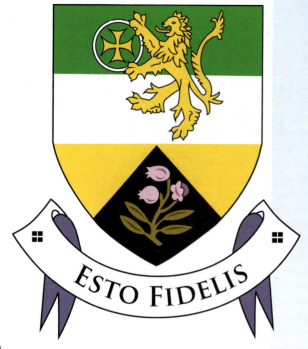

Ireland's county coats of arms usually contain symbols related to that county. Have a look at County Offaly's coat of arms, for example. Firstly, the colours, green, white and gold are those used in the Offaly flag. The gold lion is the symbol of the O'Conor Faly clan who descended from the Uí failge Kings of eastern Offaly and Leinster. The lion is holding a cross from the Book of Durrow, a famous manuscript that originates in Offaly. The flower represents the unique landscape of Offaly's boglands.

Design and Draw

Design a new coat of arms for your county using symbols which represent your county as it is today. Explain the meaning of the symbols and colours used in the new coat of arms. Write a motto for your county coat of arms. Why did you choose this motto?

Over to You

1. What is the purpose of a coat of arms?
2. Draw a picture of your county's coat of arms.
3. What colours are in your county's coat of arms? What do they represent?
4. What symbols are in the coat of arms? What do they mean?
5. Do you think the coat of arms represents the county well? Why?
6. Does your county have a motto? What is it?

County Car Registration Numbers

Since 1987, all Irish cars have used a special format for car registration plates. Firstly, it gives the last two numbers from the year, then a county code and then a number. So a car with a registration 08-D-19823 was registered in 2008 in Dublin and it was the 19,823 car to be registered that year in Dublin. Every county has its own code. Some have two. Tipperary, for example, uses TN for North Tipperary and TS for South Tipperary. Other counties like Waterford and Limerick also have two, one for the city and one for the county. The table shows all the codes.

Think and Discuss

A class investigated their teachers' car registration plates to see where the cars were from. They made a graph to show the results.

1. Which county did most of the cars come from?

Registration Codes of Teacher's Cars

Leitrim	Roscommon	Sligo	Longford	Cavan	Unknown
7	2	2	1	4	2

Why do you think that is?

2. Why do you think the counties of Roscommon, Sligo, Longford and Cavan were represented?

3. Why might the children not know what county two of the cars came from even if they had the list of codes?

4. Imagine Northern Ireland decided to join this scheme of codes. Choose a code for each of the six counties.

	County code
C	Co. Cork
CE	Co. Clare
CN	Co. Cavan
CW	Co. Carlow
D	Co. Dublin
DL	Co. Donegal
G	Co. Galway
KE	Co. Kildare
KK	Co. Kilkenny
KY	Co. Kerry
L	Limerick City
LD	Co. Longford
LH	Co. Louth
LK	Co. Limerick
LM	Co. Leitrim
LS	Co. Laois
MH	Co. Meath
MN	Co. Monaghan
MO	Co. Mayo
OY	Co. Offaly
RN	Co. Roscommon
SO	Co. Sligo
TN	North Tipperary
TS	South Tipperary
W	Waterford City
WD	Co. Waterford
WH	Co. Westmeath
WX	Co. Wexford
WW	Co. Wicklow

Lesson Wrap-Up

Visual Summary

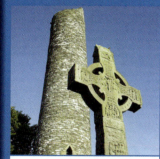

There are 32 counties in Ireland divided into four provinces: Connaught, Ulster, Munster and Leinster.

Every county in Ireland has a coat of arms. This is a design that is shaped like a shield and has many features on it. Historically, a coat of arms was the property of a family.

The 26 counties of the Republic of Ireland use a code system for their car registrations.

Review

1. **Recall**
   What is a county coat of arms?

2. **Vocabulary**
   I am a mystery word. I have eight letters, two syllables and I begin with the letter P. I mean a division of territory in Ireland.

3. **Critical Thinking**
   Identify three interesting facts about your county which make it different from other Irish counties.

4. **Be a Geographer!**
   Research a town or city outside your own county. Write a short tourist guide with information about local history, famous people from the area, top tourist attractions, natural features and what the town has to offer in terms of shops, restaurants and places to stay.

What Did I Learn?

What have I learned in this chapter?

What else would I like to know?

Where can I find this information?

Unlocking Geography • 5th Class

9 Land and Water in Ireland

What Will I Learn?

- The names and locations of some Irish rivers, lakes, mountain ranges, islands, headlands and bays.
- How to tell the differences between a river and a lake, and a bay and a headland.
- How to design a plan for making a harbour.
- Why mountains and rivers are important to people and animals.

Think and Discuss

1. Have you been anywhere in Ireland that is similar to these photographs? Where?
2. How have people used some of the natural features shown below?
3. Which photograph is the most similar to your area? Why?
4. Which photograph is your favourite? Why?

KEY VOCABULARY

bay   river settlements

mountain ranges

headland

harbour   mainland

Unlocking Geography • 5th Class

Rivers and Lakes

The map below shows some of the main rivers and lakes in Ireland. Many early settlements developed near rivers because they provided practical benefits. Early settlers used rivers for transport and travel. They could also fish and farm the fertile soil on the river banks. Some of the biggest cities and towns in Ireland, including Dublin, Cork, Galway and Limerick, all began as river settlements. Ireland also has many lakes which are used for fishing and boating, which add greatly to Ireland's appeal as a tourist destination.

Rivers and lakes have an important place too in Irish folklore and history. According to legend, Fionn Mac Cumhaill was once fighting with a Scottish giant. He grabbed a piece of earth in anger, to throw at the giant, and the hole left behind became Lough Neagh. There are many other Irish myths and legends about lakes and rivers.

Geographical Investigation Skills

1. Name your local rivers and lakes.
2. Are your local rivers and lakes used by animals?
3. How do people use the rivers and lakes in your local area?

Design and Draw

Design a leaflet advertising your local lake as a tourist attraction.

Map Skills

1. Name the biggest lake in Ireland.
2. Which counties does the River Shannon flow through?
3. Where is the source of the River Shannon?
4. Name the rivers in Galway, Cork and Dublin.

Mountains

Ireland is very popular with hill walkers and mountain climbers because there are a range of mountains to choose from, many offering spectacular views and scenery. Mountains can be found in many different parts of the country. The Blue Stack Mountains are a major mountain range located in County Donegal, in the North of Ireland. On the Eastern side of the country, the Wicklow Mountains have a peak that measures 926 metres. This mountain range also has a number of well-known valleys like Avoca, Aughrim, Glendalough and Avonmore. Other impressive mountain ranges include the Comeragh and Knockmealdown mountains. The Knockmealdown mountains have seven peaks, the highest being 795 metres tall. The Comeragh mountains in Waterford have a peak of 792 metres and a number of cirques and corries. The Galtee mountains between Limerick and Tipperary also have a number of corries as well as lakes and morraines, left behind from glaciation. The Macgillycuddy's Reeks mountain range, on the Iveragh Peninsula of County Kerry, contain the highest mountain in Ireland. Carauntoohil is 1,041 metres high and is the highest point in the Republic of Ireland.

Did You Know?
The mountain hare is well-known for making its habitat in upland and mountain areas but some animals are not so famous. If you take a good look around a mountain in Ireland, you could spot a viviparous lizard!

CHECKPOINT

1. Why is Ireland a popular destination for hill walkers and mountain climbers?
2. Name a major mountain range in the North of Ireland.
3. Name two valleys in the Wicklow mountains.
4. How many peaks are in the Knockmealdown mountains?
5. Name the highest mountain in Ireland and say where it is located.

Unlocking Geography • 5th Class

Croagh Patrick

Croagh Patrick is a mountain in County Mayo, overlooking Clew Bay. It has one of the highest peaks in the west of Ireland, rising to 750 metres. Croagh Patrick is considered by Catholics to be a very holy mountain. It is said that Ireland's patron saint, Saint Patrick, fasted for 40 days on the summit of Croagh Patrick in AD 441. Every year, a pilgrimage takes place there on the last Sunday in July. Thousands of people of all ages make the trek up the rocky mountainside, some in their bare feet. During the pilgrimage, a priest says prayers, and when the pilgrims reach the top of the mountain, they celebrate mass in a chapel.

The tradition of climbing Croagh Patrick is over 5,000 years old, in the past people gathered on it to celebrate the beginning of harvest season. Other pilgrimages take place at Croagh Patrick on the last Friday of July and August 15th. The mountain attracts over one million visitors including historians, archaeologists, hill walkers, mountain climbers and pilgrims.

Think and Discuss

1. Why do people walk barefoot up Croagh Patrick, do you think?
2. What is the difference between a mountain and a hill?
3. Why, do you think, are historians and archaeologists interested in visiting Croagh Patrick?

Geographical Investigation Skills

1. Using your atlas, find out the locations for the following mountain ranges: Slieve Mish, Mourne Mountains and Derryveagh Mountains.
2. Using the internet or an encyclopaedia, name the five highest mountain peaks in Ireland.

The Key to Literacy

Have you ever heard of hillwalking? Hillwalking is a hike up hills and mountains and it is very popular in Ireland. Write a paragraph advertising a hike up your local mountain. Do not forget to add in interesting things to see along the way.

Bays, Islands and Headlands

Bays, islands and headlands are important natural features. A bay is an area of seashore that curves inwards and is surrounded by land on three sides. Harbours are often built near bays. A headland is a piece of the mainland that juts out into the sea. An island is a piece of land surrounded by water. Ireland itself is an island and there are many small islands dotted around the Irish coast.

Blog

Hi! My name is Breffni and I live on the island of Inisheer. It is the smallest of the three Aran Islands in Galway Bay. People also live on the other two islands. I love living here because it feels different from living on the mainland. The island is small so we can walk from place to place, but most people have a car too. Throughout the year, but especially in the summer months, tourists come over on boats to visit the island. Some of them are surprised that we still speak Irish here every day. Some people come to study the language. There are a few hotels and hostels here, but a lot of people come for a day trip and go back again on the boat that evening. Only about 300 people live on the island. It is sometimes fun to take the small plane to Connemara Regional Airport and then to go to Galway for shopping and a trip to the cinema. The winters can be harsh on the island, but my family loves snuggling up in front of the fire during a storm!

CHECKPOINT

1. What is a bay?
2. What is an island?
3. What is a headland?
4. What attracts visitors to the island of Inisheer?

Think and Discuss

1. What would you like about living on an island? What would you dislike about it?
2. What kinds of jobs do you think people on this island would work at?

Map Skills

1. Which is the biggest island off Ireland's coast? What county is it in? Do people live on this island?
2. What is the nearest bay to you called? How did it get its name?
3. Which island is closest to where you live? How did it get its name?
4. What headland is nearest to you? How did it get its name?
5. Listen to a radio weather forecast. Does it mention headlands in Ireland? Which ones? Why do you think it mentions them?

Lesson Wrap-Up

Visual Summary

Ireland has a number of lakes, rivers, mountains, bays, headlands and islands.

There are many important rivers in Ireland, many of our cities and towns were founded on rivers.

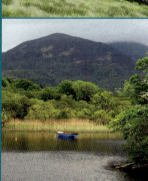
The tallest mountain in Ireland is Carrauntoohil in County Kerry. Irish mountains are very popular with hill walkers and climbers.

What Did I Learn?

What have I learned in this chapter?

What else would I like to know?

Where can I find this information?

Review

1. **Recall**
   Name two animals that live in Irish mountains.

2. **Vocabulary**
   The word 'headland' is a compound word, which means it is made up of two words, 'head' and 'land'. Can you name four more compound words?

3. **Critical Thinking**
   Evaluate the reasons why some of Ireland's biggest towns and cities were founded on rivers. Why were these locations suitable for early settlers?

4. **Be a Geographer!**
   Find a bay in Ireland that has no harbour and design a plan to build one. What kinds of things would you expect to find at a harbour? Who would use it?

10 Travelling and Commuting to Work

What Will I Learn?

- How to plan journeys using different forms of transport.
- Advantages and disadvantages of living in a commuter town.
- Arguments for and against bypassing a town.
- About the national roads and motorways of Ireland.

Think and Discuss

1. Describe what you can see in each photograph.
2. What do these photographs all have in common?
3. Which of these types of transport are available in your locality?
4. Which type of transport do you prefer to travel on? Why?
5. Which type of transport, do you think, is best for the environment?

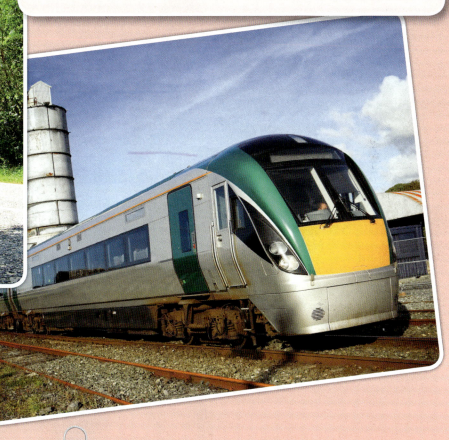

 KEY VOCABULARY

commuters   motorways
Quality Bus Corridors
passing trade   bypass
congested

Travelling to Work

In Ireland, many people have to travel long distances to get to work. We call people who travel long distances to work, commuters. Commuters use various means to travel to and from their workplaces. Many use public transport. Public transport refers to travel services such as buses, trains and metro systems. Although Ireland offers numerous transport services, many people feel there are still not enough to meet the needs of commuters. For example, the Luas (a tram system) and DART (a train that serves the greater Dublin area) only travel in County Dublin and north County Wicklow. Many people have no other choice but to drive to work. Read the blogs of three commuters and find out what kind of transport they take to work.

Well, I am just home after my daily two hour journey from work. My name is Gareth and I am getting sick of travelling up and down to my job in Dublin city. I live in Carnew, in County Wicklow and the only way I can get to work on time is by car. There is only one bus from Carnew to Dublin and that's at 9.40 a.m. and I start at 9 a.m. My nearest train station is Gorey but that's a 20 minute drive and there's usually nowhere to leave my car for the day. With fuel prices rising all the time, my commute is proving very costly. I would definitely take the bus if there was one available. Until then, I'll be driving to Dublin every day of the week.

Hi, Rebecca here. I live in Newtown Park Avenue near Blackrock in Dublin and work in the city centre. It used to take me nearly an hour to get home from work until Dublin Bus started to use Quality Bus Corridors (QBC). This has given Dublin Buses priority traffic signals and designated areas on the road. Thanks to QBC, my commute is now only half an hour! I love sitting back listening to music and passing the cars by! I used to have to leave for work at about 7.30 a.m. every morning, now I get an extra half hour in bed.

Hi, my name is Amy. There's always a rush in our house in the mornings. I have to get to Woodlawn train station by 7.39 a.m. or the train is gone! I usually get the train three times a week because I don't need to be at my job in Galway until 9 a.m. and the train gets in at 8:20 a.m. The rest of the week, I drive. In general, I prefer not to drive to work because the traffic queues can be very frustrating and I know that I could be relaxing with a nice cup of coffee on the train. In fact, whenever I do take the train, I feel much more prepared for work.

CHECKPOINT

1. How does Gareth feel about his commute? Why?
2. Why does Rebecca enjoy commuting?
3. Explain Quality Bus Corridors.
4. Why does Amy sometimes drive to work?

Using Public Transport

Shane Barrett has to commute to work every day. He lives in Mullingar and works in Dublin and so relies on the bus to get to work each day for 9 a.m. Have a look at the bus timetable and answer the questions.

MULLINGAR - DUBLIN					
	Departure Time				
Mullingar	05:30	06:30	07:00	07:30	08:00
Kinnegad	05:40	06:40	07:10	07:40	08:10
Clonard	05:45	06:45	07:15	07:45	08:15
Moyvalley	05:50	06:50	07:20	07:50	08:20
Enfield	05:55	06:55	07:25	07:55	08:25
Maynooth	06:10	07:10	07:40	08:10	08:40
	Arrival Time				
Dublin	06:40	07:40	08:10	08:40	09:10

Geographical Investigation Skills

1. How many buses travel from Mullingar to Dublin and arrive before 9 a.m?

2. What stops does a bus from Mullingar to Dublin make?

3. What is the earliest time Shane can get to Dublin? Along what roads do you think the bus travels? Give reasons for your answer.

4. A train also runs from Mullingar to Dublin. Which form of transport, do you think, would be most reliable? Why?

Did You Know?

The first railway line in Ireland ran from Dublin to Kingstown, now called Dun Laoghaire. It opened in 1834. It was one of the earliest commuter railways in the world.

Commuter Towns

A commuter town (also known as a dormitory town) is a town where most of the inhabitants travel to a different town or city to go to work. Commuter towns develop when people cannot afford to live in the place where they work and have to find a cheaper house somewhere else.

Advantages and Disadvantages of Commuter Towns

Commuter towns offer more affordable housing than cities and people often move to these towns from different places. As a result, there can be a good sense of community with new schools, shops and community centres opening. Some well-populated commuter towns have convenient access to important services like doctors and dentists. Others, however, lack services and recreational facilities and so people have to travel substantial distances for them.

In some commuter towns, roads are improved or a bypass is built around the town to allow for better traffic flow. New bus and train services are also introduced to meet the demands of busy commuters. However, not all commuter towns have suitable roads or sufficient bus and train services. These towns can become congested with traffic at peak times, in the morning and evening when people are travelling to and from work.

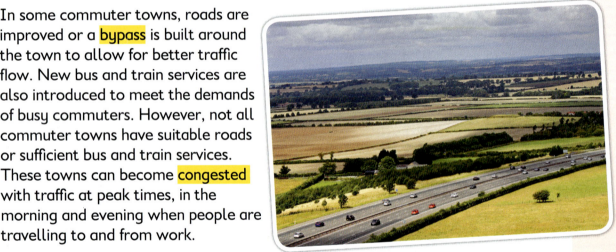

The Key to Literacy
The word commuter has three syllables. What other words in this section have three syllables? Create a list of ten words related to transport that have three or more syllables.

CHECKPOINT

1. What is a commuter town?
2. How are commuter towns created?
3. What are the advantages and disadvantages of commuter towns?

The Bypass Debate

Sometimes people have different opinions about whether or not a town should be bypassed. Read the blogs below to discover two different opinions about the positive and negative aspects of a bypass.

Laura from Castleisland, Co. Kerry

Hi my name is Laura. I go to college in Dublin. I used to take the train home at weekends but recently I got a car. I thought my journey would be a lot easier now but I feel really frustrated. After I leave the motorway, I come to Adare in Limerick. It is a bottleneck town, especially at 6 o'clock on a Friday evening. I can spend up to 40 minutes in lines of traffic. This adds a lot of time to my journey home. I never stop off at any of the shops here because I don't want to lose my place in the traffic queue. Castleisland, where I'm from, used to be a bottleneck too. It was really difficult for locals trying to get home from work and school when the town was congested with traffic. Our bypass opened in October 2010, linking the N23 Killarney road to the N21 Limerick road. It cost €35 million to build and stretches over 5.4 km. Thanks to the bypass, over 60% of traffic has been diverted away from the town centre. I think Adare would really benefit from a bypass too.

John from Adare, Co. Limerick

Hi, my name is John and I own a petrol station and a pub in the town of Adare. A while back, there were talks of building a bypass around the town. Myself and many of the other locals objected. A bypass would be disastrous for the town as we would lose a great deal of our passing trade. Many tourists heading to the south of the country pass through here. If they were to avoid the town by using a bypass, I know my shop would be negatively affected. Many people stop for petrol and a cup of coffee after a long drive on the motorway and lots of tour buses stop off at my pub for lunch. I hope the town is never bypassed – there would be too many drawbacks for the locals!

Think and Discuss

Based on what you have read, do you think a bypass would be a good idea for the town of Adare? Why?/Why not?

Design and Draw

The government have announced plans to bypass your nearest town. Do you agree or disagree with their plan? Make a poster to show your opinion.

Deciding Your Route

The map of Ireland below shows all the national roads and motorways. These roads are considered to be the best quality roads in the country. Many of these roads are used by commuters to travel to work.

Map Skills

1. Name Ireland's motorways.
2. What is the closest motorway to your home?
3. To get from Carlow to Dublin, take the M9 and the M7. Then join the N7 into Dublin. Use a similar sentence to describe each of the following routes:
   - Letterkenny to Castleblaney
   - Waterford to Arklow
   - Thurles to Limerick
   - Galway to Sligo

Lesson Wrap-Up

Visual Summary

People who travel long distances to work are called commuters. Commuters use cars or public transport like the luas, buses or trains to get to work.

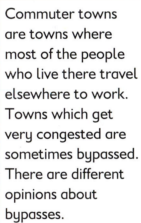

Commuter towns are towns where most of the people who live there travel elsewhere to work. Towns which get very congested are sometimes bypassed. There are different opinions about bypasses.

The national roads and motorways in Ireland are considered to be the best quality roads in the country.

Review

1. **Recall**
   What name is given to people who travel long distances to work?

2. **Vocabulary**
   Look at the word transport. 'Trans' is a prefix. Can you think of other words with the prefix 'trans'? List them.

3. **Critical Thinking**
   Why, do you think, does the government prefer that people do not drive to work?

4. **Be a Geographer!**
   A new town needs to be built to cope with the increasing population. It is estimated that 20,000 people will live in the town. What services does the town need? Draw a plan of the new town labelling the services, e.g. schools and parks. Remember to include transport.

What Did I Learn?

What have I learned in this chapter?

What else would I like to know?

Where can I find this information?

11 Fishing in Ireland

What Will I Learn?

- Why Ireland is a popular fishing destination.
- The many species of fish that live in Irish waters.
- What a fishing village in Ireland offers to tourists.
- What it would be like to work in the fishing industry.

Think and Discuss

1. Describe what you see in each photograph.
2. Do any of the places in the photographs look similar to your locality?
3. Have you ever taken part in any of the water sport activities shown in the photographs?
4. Which is your favourite photograph? Why?
5. Which is your least favourite photograph? Why?

KEY VOCABULARY

species abundant
distinctive native scenic
ecological reefs

Unlocking Geography • 5th Class

Fishing in Ireland

Ireland is a great place for fishing. Here are some reasons why.

1. Ireland is an island with a very high ratio of water to land. It is surrounded by the North Sea, Irish Sea and Atlantic Ocean.
2. It has a coastline of 3,000 km, 14,000 km of fish-bearing rivers and 12,000 lakes, which are home to many salmon and trout species.
3. The inshore waters of Ireland are warmed by the North Atlantic Drift, making them the right temperature for a huge variety of marine life.
4. The Irish climate of moderate summers, mild winters and plentiful rainfall is good for fishermen who get many chances to take to the seas.
5. The climate is suitable for both cold and warm water fish species, so Ireland benefits by having many different types of fish.

Whatever the Weather

Many fishermen and tourists come to Ireland on fishing holidays. They know that our climate has just the right amount of heat, cold and rain to make for an ideal fishing experience. Thanks to the mild temperatures and high rainfall, lakes are of good ecological quality and there are waters to suit fish species from around the world. Fresh warm water carp, cold water cod, North Atlantic salmon and Mediterranean bass are all attracted to Irish waters. Good news for those of us who love to fish!

Think and Discuss

Many tourists come to Ireland for fishing. Can you think of other reasons why tourists love to visit Ireland?

CHECKPOINT

1. Give three reasons why Ireland is ideal for fishing.
2. Name three types of fish found in Irish waters.
3. How are the inshore waters of Ireland kept warm?

Design and Draw

Design an advertisement that could be included in a magazine to promote Ireland as a top fishing destination.

Downings

An Irish Fishing Village

The village of Downings is in County Donegal, the most northern county in the Republic of Ireland. It is very popular with tourists because it offers some of the best sea-fishing experiences in the country and has beautiful scenery.

There are a variety of fish to be found near Downings pier and in the **reefs** around Tory island, which are famous for large pollock and conger eel. Mulroy Bay is a great place to fish, even in stormy weather, as there are plenty of ray, plaice, turbot and dogfish. Downings even has shark fishing from July to September!

Visitors to Downings can also explore ship wrecks off the Donegal coast in an activity known as 'wreck fishing'. It is the perfect place for experienced fishermen, but is also an ideal setting for people who are new to fishing. There are lots of companies and skippers who can teach people how to fish.

CHECKPOINT

1. What attracts tourists to Downings?
2. Name three types of fish found in Downings.
3. How does Downings offer a unique fishing experience?

Think and Discuss

Think of some jobs that might be in the Downings area as a result of the successful fishing industry there. What other types of industry do you think may be popular in Downings? Why?

Did You Know?

The largest blue shark ever caught in Downings weighed 76 kg.

Research and Write It

Research another Irish fishing village and write about what the place is like and the kinds of activities it offers visitors.

Fish in Irish Waters

There are a wide variety of different fish species in Ireland. You can read about some of the most common types below.

Freshwater Fish

Ireland is home to a wide variety of freshwater fish. These fish live in lakes and rivers, rather than the salty waters of seas and oceans. Freshwater fish

are among the most nutritious fish that we can eat. Some of the most common types in Ireland are bream, perch, salmon, trout, pike, eel and carp.

Bream is a fish found in many rivers and lakes around Ireland, including the Erne, Shannon, Bann and lakes in Cavan, Monaghan, Cork, Clare and Meath. Young bream fish are very slimy, grey on top and silver on the sides, with large grey fins. Adult bream are a bronze colour and have very dark fins.

Perch is a fish often found in the River Barrow and Lower Lough Erne. A perch is easy to recognise because of its green colour, vertical black stripes and red tail. It also has sharp spines on its fins and gills. The salmon is a native Irish freshwater fish found in Irish rivers and loughs from spring to autumn. Fishermen looking for salmon often visit scenic fisheries, such as the Moy in Mayo and Munster Blackwater in Cork. Salmon have silvery skin with spotted back and fins.

Brown trout and rainbow trout are found in rivers, loughs and estuaries all over Ireland. The brown trout is a native Irish species. Trout have different colour and patterns to match their environment. A trout's fin has no spine.

▲ *Salmon*

Saltwater Fish

The sea waters around Ireland are abundant in fish species. So much so, that Ireland is considered one of the best sea-angling destinations in the world. There are around 80 species of fish living in Irish seas. Some of the most popular saltwater fish include cod, bass, turbot and pollack.

Cod live in the cold waters of the Atlantic. They have dull grey-speckled skin and a distinctive feature called a 'barbel', which hangs from the lower jaw.

▲ Cod

Cod can be found year-round on most Irish coasts, in large estuaries and areas of shingle and sand. They are considered to be very nutritious, in particular for the oil in their livers – 'cod-liver oil' – which is a rich source of vitamins A and D.

Bass is a protected fish species that is very popular with sea anglers. A bass fish has a spiked dorsal fin and a forked tail. Bass are commonly found in piers, estuaries and rocky promontories. They are most common in southern parts of the country.

Turbot are large flat fish with diamond-shaped bodies. They have brown spotted bodies that blend in with the ocean floor. They eat many other fish and can grow to be quite large; some have reached 1 m in length and 22 kg in weight.

Pollack are commonly found in reefs and over areas of rough ground. They are usually brown in colour and have protruding jaws. The Pollack is a long fish, dark green in colour. It can grow to over 1 metre in length and weigh up to 16 kg.

▲ Turbot

CHECKPOINT

1. How many species of fish do we have in Ireland?
2. What type of fish is bream?
3. How would you recognise a cod?
4. Where in Ireland might you go if you want to catch a salmon?
5. Name a type of trout that can be found all over Ireland.

The Key to Literacy

Think of another word for each of the following:
- species
- distinctive
- scenic

Design and Draw

Design a menu for a fish restaurant. Include some nice fish dishes that you have tried in the past or create a new fish dish of your own!

A Career in Fishing

The Weekly Catch newspaper has an advertisement for a job working on a fishing boat. Read the advertisement and answer the questions.

Work Available

The Weekly Catch

Job description

You will spend much of your time in a fishing boat on the water. Your job will involve hauling in fish and bringing it back quickly for our local market. At first, you will be fishing for crab, but your job will change over time and you will do more varied fishing. You will be working alongside a captain and deckhand in your first year, but may later become a captain, mate, deckhand or labourer.

Requirements

You will have interest in fish and enjoy life at sea. You will also need to be ready to spend some long, often difficult, hours at sea.

Education

No formal education is needed but you should be good at finding and hooking fish! If you hope to reach a high position on larger vessels, you may need additional training.

Related careers

Similar careers include: fish hatchery, aquaculture work, fishing and hunting guide, game warden/inspector, merchant marine officer or coast guard.

CHECKPOINT

1. List three skills needed to do this job.
2. What activities does this job involve? Give three examples.
3. What are the physical requirements needed for the job?

Think and Discuss

Would you like to apply for this job? Why/Why not?

Lesson Wrap-Up

Visual Summary

Fishing is an important part of Ireland's tourism industry. Our climate, large coastline and abundance of rivers and lakes mean our waters are suited to fish.

Downings is a popular tourist village in County Donegal. Downings offers some of the best sea fishing experiences and is a favourite destination for tourists.

Coarse fish, sea fish, salmon and trout are among the most common types of fish found in Irish waters. People who work in the fishing industry need to have an interest in fish and enjoy being at sea.

Review

1. **Recall**
   Name two kinds of trout found in Ireland.

2. **Vocabulary**
   List synonyms for the word 'abundant'.

3. **Critical Thinking**
   Imagine a fish in your area was being over fished. What steps would you take to stop this from happening?

4. **Be a Geographer!**
   Investigate the best places in Ireland to catch salmon or trout. Research some rivers and loughs which are popular for these kinds of fish. Make a table to show your findings. Include information on the best times of year to make a catch.

What Did I Learn?

What have I learned in this chapter?

What else would I like to know?

Where can I find this information?

12 Weather and Climate

What Will I Learn?

- The difference between weather and climate.
- How weather and climate affect Ireland and the world.
- About world climate zones.
- About climate conditions in some other parts of the world and how they affect life there.

Think and Discuss

1. What kinds of weather do you see in these photographs?
2. Which of these photographs would you most associate with typical Irish weather? Why?
3. Which of these photographs would you least associate with typical Irish weather? Why?
4. Which photographs show the weather having a positive effect on people?
5. Which photographs show the weather having a negative effect on people?

KEY VOCABULARY

latitude

air pressure

tundra

aspect

altitude

Antarctic

What is Weather?

A simple definition of weather is short-term (daily) changes in the temperature around us. However, weather is made up of many different parts: temperature, precipitation, wind and air pressure. Temperature is how hot or cold the air is. Precipitation is water that falls from the sky in the form of rain, hail, sleet or snow. Another part that makes-up the weather is wind, which can be anything from a mild breeze to a strong tornado. The pressure in the air is also a key part of weather and affects all of these other parts. Simply put, air pressure is the pressure that air applies to the Earth's surface. Weather also involves sunshine, visibility, cloud and humidity.

Irish Weather

To find out information about the weather, we can watch weather reports, read a newspaper or go online. Before we had meteorologists, the scientists who study the weather, people used traditional sayings and proverbs to help predict the weather. Examples include; 'Rain before seven, fine by eleven', 'Flies will swarm before a storm' and 'If crows fly low, winds going to blow; if crows fly high, winds going to die'.

Met Éireann is the Irish national weather service which provides the country with up-to-the-minute weather forecasts and warnings.

Met Éireann also keeps very detailed records of the weather in various parts of Ireland each year. This allows them to compare and contrast the weather in various regions and to check if Irish weather shows significant change over the years.

CHECKPOINT

1. Name four elements of weather.
2. What is air pressure?
3. What does Met Éireann do?

What is Climate?

Sometimes you may hear people referring to the climate of a place. Climate is something quite different to weather. The climate is the common, average weather conditions in a particular place over a long period of time (for example, more than 30 years). In other words, climate is the long-term pattern of weather in any part of the world.

Over to You

1. Can you think of any other weather sayings? Do you think there is any truth to them?
2. Look at the Met Éireann website. They have a section for past weather that is broken down into monthly reports for various areas in Ireland. These areas have weather stations where special equipment takes readings of temperature, rainfall, wind speed, air pressure and humidity. Find some monthly reports on a weather station near you. What does it tell you about the weather in that area? How do you think a weather station measures rainfall?

Climate Zones

There are several climate zones in the world.

Polar – This zone is very cold and dry all year.

Temperate – This zone has cold winters and mild summers.

Mediterranean – This zone has mild winters and hot, dry summers.

Mountains – This zone is also known as the tundra zone and is very cold all year.

Arid – This zone is dry and hot all year.

Tropical – This zone is hot and wet all year.

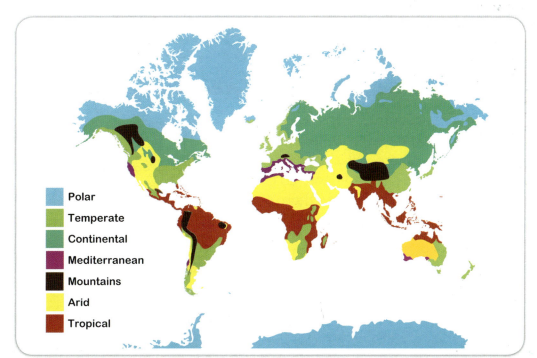

Climate Factors

Latitude is the distance north or south that a place is from the equator. Look at a map of the world – the line on the map running around the middle of the Earth is called the equator. It divides the Earth into two halves, a northern hemisphere and a southern hemisphere. As you move further away from the equator, north or south, the temperatures will get lower.

Altitude is the height that a place is above sea level or above the surface of the land. The higher a piece of land is, the lower the temperature.

Wind is air blowing from place to place. If an area experiences winds blowing in from a hot area, the temperature will increase.

If a place experiences winds blowing in from a cold area, the temperature will drop.

Aspect is the direction that a mountain slope is facing. Mountain slopes that face the sun are warmer than those that face away from the sun. South facing slopes in the northern hemisphere are usually warm. North facing slopes in the southern hemisphere are also usually warm.

Think and Discuss

1. Which climate zone is Ireland in? Does Irish weather match the description of this zone?

2. Which climate zones are the most different from Ireland's climate zone?

3. Choose three countries in the southern hemisphere and three countries in the northern hemisphere. Which climate zones are they in? What factors do you think might affect the climate there?

4. Where is Ireland in relation to the equator? Give three reasons why it could be good to live near the equator? Give three reasons why it could be bad to live near the equator.

Did You Know?
Warm and cold ocean or sea currents can affect the climate in a place in much the same way as warm or cool winds.

Three World Climates

Rainforest Climate

The tropical rainforest climate is very hot and wet. This type of climate experiences daily thunderstorms. Trees are evergreen and have large, wide leaves to catch the sun's light. The trees are incredibly tall and their leaves reach high up into the sky, creating a canopy. The canopy lets very little light reach the ground. Because of this, there are hardly any plants on the forest floor. Rainforests are home to the widest variety of plant and animal life on earth. One country that has huge areas of rainforest is Brazil, in South America.

Mediterranean Climate

Countries that have a Mediterranean climate have hot summers, mild winters and sunshine all year round. In winter, temperatures rarely drop below 5°C. Strong winds can cause great damage to crops and can also increase the risk of forest fires. Various plants have adapted themselves to the features of a Mediterranean climate. Take, for example, the olive tree. It has rough leaves and chunky bark and these help it cope with the extreme heat and dryness of the summer time. Mediterranean countries such as Italy produce many different citrus fruits, such as lemons and oranges, as these fruits grow very well in the heat.

13 Latvia

What Will I Learn?
- About the geography of Latvia. How to compare Ireland and Latvia.
- About the city of Riga.
- About Latvia's open air museum.
- About Latvians in Ireland.

Think and Discuss

1. Describe what you see in each photograph.
2. Which photographs are similar to places in Ireland?
3. Which photographs are different to places in Ireland?
4. Which is your favourite photograph? Why?
5. Would you like to visit this country? Why?

KEY VOCABULARY

Baltic States

Laima Clock

Latvian

ethnographic

Freedom Monument

Unlocking Geography • 5th Class 103

Putting Latvia on the Map

Latvia is a country in northeastern Europe. It is bordered by Russia, Belarus, Lithuania and Estonia and lies on the shores of the Baltic Sea and Gulf of Riga. Riga is the capital of Latvia and has the largest population of any Latvian city. Around one-third of the agricultural land in Latvia is used to grow crops like rye, wheat, barley and oats. Vegetables like onions, carrots, potatoes and sugar beets are grown for export. A smaller portion of the land is used for livestock farming. Fish like pike, bream, eel and perch are caught in the Baltic Sea to be sold within Latvia. Latvia has many exports; the main exports are textiles, wood products, metals and vegetables.

Visitors to Latvia enjoy its attractive lakes and coastline, historic castles and monasteries. There is a rich culture of song and dance in Latvia, with many colourful festivals taking place in different regions of the country. A festival called Jāņi takes place every summer to celebrate the summer solstice. There are bonfires and plenty of food and drink. Folk songs called dainas are a special part of Latvian culture. Dainas are quite short, no longer than four lines and are sung to tell stories of love, family and legends.

CHECKPOINT

1. Which countries border Latvia?
2. Name three crops which are grown in Latvia.
3. What are the main products exported from Latvia?
4. Explain what a daina is in Latvian culture.

Did You Know?
- Latvia is one of the three Baltic States. The other two are Estonia and Lithuania.
- Until 1991, Latvia was part of the Union of Soviet Socialist Republics (U.S.S.R.) or Soviet Union.

Ireland and Latvia Fact File

	Ireland	Latvia
Flag		
Official Name	Éire; Ireland	Latvijas Republika (Republic of Latvia)
Continent	Europe	Europe
EU Member Since	1973	2004
Political System	Republic	Republic
Size	70,273 km²	64,589 km²
Capital City	Dublin	Riga
Population (2011 est.)	4,606,000	2,217,000
Main Languages	Irish; English	Latvian; Russian; Romany; Yiddish
Currency	euro	lats
Main Religion(s)	Roman Catholic; Church of Ireland	Lutheran; Roman Catholic; Eastern Orthodox

Think and Discuss

1. What are the similarities and differences between Ireland and Latvia?
2. Compare and contrast the flags of Ireland and Latvia. Why do you think those colours and designs were chosen for each country?

Over to You
1. Find out three other interesting facts about Latvia.
2. Plan a journey from Riga to your locality using any type of transport.

The Key to Literacy
Write down the steps that you would take if you were to go to a library to do research on the country of Latvia.

Did You Know?
The first ever use of an evergreen tree in Christmas celebrations took place in Riga in 1510.

Exploring Riga

Riga is the capital city of Latvia. Although there are around 77 towns and cities in Latvia, the majority of the population lives in Riga. Most Latvian businesses, companies and government offices are also located in the capital. Riga has over 50 museums. Riga Castle was built in 1330 and now houses the president of Latvia. The city also has many famous monuments and buildings. The most famous of these is the ==Freedom Monument==. It was erected in 1935 in memory of the Latvian people who were deported to Siberia during Soviet times. Another monument is the ==Laima Clock==, which is a very famous meeting place in the city.

▲ *Riga Castle*

▲ *The Freedom Monument in Riga*

▲ *The centre of Riga*

Think and Discuss

1. What do you think the phrase 'Soviet times' refers to?
2. What would you most like to visit in Riga? Why?
3. Do we have any monuments like the Freedom Monument in Ireland?
4. The Laima Clock is a popular meeting point in Riga. Is there a special meeting place in your locality? Why do people meet there?

Did You Know?
The most popular brand of chocolate in Latvia is called Laima, after the Laima Clock.

Over to You
1. How many towns and cities are there in Latvia? Is that more or less than Ireland?
2. The Latvian president lives in Riga Castle. Where does the Irish president live?

Latvia's Open Air Museum

The Latvian Ethnographic Open Air Museum is one of the oldest open air museums in Europe, located in a pine forest in Riga. It was established in 1924 and consists of 118 historical Latvian buildings, some dating back to the 17th century. Buildings were relocated and reconstructed to show what life was like in Latvia in years gone by. There are farmsteads that belonged to farmers, craftsmen and fishermen, with authentic tools and furnished households.

The museum holds exhibitions of jobs and crafts that were popular in the past. Like Ireland, many ancient crafts have since vanished. Demonstrations of blacksmithing, weaving, woodcarving, woodturning and beekeeping all take place. In fact, there are over 140,000 different things to see in this museum.

There is an annual summer market, where craftspeople from all over Latvia and other countries exhibit and sell their products. At weekends, visitors can watch craftsmen doing traditional work in the farmsteads. During Christmas, the museum hosts a traditional Latvian Christmas party with parades, mulled wine, sauerkraut and sleigh rides.

Think and Discuss

1. Do you know of a similar museum in Ireland? Find where it is located on a map of Ireland.
2. Describe a market that is held close to your locality.
3. If an open air museum opened in your locality, what would be in it? Why?

Did You Know?
The word 'ethnographic' describes the study of human cultures.

Design and Draw
Make a poster to advertise an event that will take place in the Open Air Museum. Choose an event which happens at a specific time of year e.g. summer or winter.

Latvians in Ireland

There are many Latvian people who have come to live and work in Ireland in recent years. From 1995 to 2007, Ireland's economy was booming. When a country's economy is booming it means that there are usually a lot of jobs to be had and the people living in that country have plenty of money to spend.

At that time, large numbers of Latvian people came to Ireland to work. It was difficult for them to find jobs at home, and Ireland offered them a better chance of finding employment. One of the jobs that many Latvian people did in Ireland was to pick mushrooms.

They could earn many times the amount of money in Ireland that they would be paid in Latvia for doing the same work. Jobs like picking mushrooms involved hard work and long hours. Some Latvian people chose to settle down in Ireland, but many wanted to save up money and go home again to their families. Latvia became part of the European Union in 2004. This made it easier for Latvian people to find work in Ireland and in other parts of Europe.

CHECKPOINT

1. What job did many Latvian people come to do in Ireland?
2. Why did they choose to come to Ireland to work?
3. Between what years was Ireland's economy booming?

Research and Write It

Imagine that you are a Latvian person working in Ireland today. From what you know about Latvia write a letter to a family member, talking about the things you miss about Latvia. Also talk about the differences that you are noticing between Ireland and Latvia.

Lesson Wrap-Up

Visual Summary

Latvia is a country in Europe. It is one of the Baltic states and has a coastline on the Baltic sea. It is bordered by Lithuania, Estonia, Russia and Belarus.

Riga is the capital city of Latvia. It contains many important buildings and landmarks, such as Riga Castle and the Freedom Monument.

Latvia is home to one of the oldest and largest open air museums in Europe. The ethnographic museum has lots of historical buildings, some dating back to the 17th century. Festivals and markets often take place in the museum.

What Did I Learn?
What have I learned in this chapter?

What else would I like to know?

Where can I find this information?

Review

1. **Recall**
   When did Latvia join the European Union?

2. **Vocabulary**
   A person who comes from Latvia is called 'Latvian'. What other nationalities are formed by giving an 'n' ending to the country name? Make a list.

3. **Critical Thinking**
   Outline the main reasons you would give to a Latvian person who was considering coming to Ireland for a holiday. What would they find different and interesting in Ireland? What would make them feel at home?

4. **Be a Geographer!**
   Find out what people around you know about Latvia. Make a list of ten questions that you could ask family members or friends. Summarise your findings and design a poster that will inform Irish people about Latvia.

Glossary

A

abseiling
a leisure activity whereby an experienced climber lowers himself/herself down a steep mountainside, cliff, building or bridge by sliding down a rope.

abundant
present in great quantity; plentiful.

accessible
relating to something that is easy to gain access or entry to, e.g. a building.

air pressure
force applied to the Earth's surface by the weight of the air above the surface – see also atmospheric pressure.

altitude
the height of something, especially land, above sea level.

amenities
a pleasant feature or service that people in the area may use.

anemometer
an instrument used for reading and recording wind speed.

Antarctic
the area around the South Pole.

aspect
the direction that a mountain slope is facing.

atmospheric pressure
force applied to the Earth's surface by the weight of the air above the surface – see also air pressure.

axis
relating to the Earth's axis – an imaginary line that goes through the Earth's centre from North Pole to South Pole, around which the Earth spins.

B

Baltic States
term used to describe three countries that border the Baltic Sea in Northern Europe; Latvia, Estonia and Lithuania.

barometer
an instrument used to measure atmospheric pressure.

bay
an area of seashore that curves inwards and is surrounded by land on three sides.

bypass
a road designed to take traffic around a busy or over-crowded town.

C

car registration numbers
the numbers on licence plates that identify registered cars.

coat of arms
a design shaped like a shield with many decorative features, which represents a specific county in Ireland.

commuters
people who travel long distances to get to work.

congested
relating to a town that is overcrowded with cars and as a result has traffic queues and delays.

core
the central part of the Earth.

county town
the biggest town in a county.

crust
the outer layer of the earth.

D

degrade
relating to the breakdown of waste material.

dignity
a sense of self-respect and pride.

discrimination
relating to treating some people differently or unfairly because of their gender, race, age, sex, etc.

distinctive
unique or recognisable.

diversity
variety.

drainage system
a system of drains for carrying away excess water.

E

ecological
environmental or natural.

economy
a system of producing and managing a country's material wealth.

ethnographic
relating to the study of human cultures.

F

fishmonger
a shopkeeper who sells fish.

forecast
a prediction about how the weather is going to be in given areas.

Freedom Monument
a famous monument in Latvia's capital city of Riga in memory of the Latvian people who were deported to Siberia during Soviet times.

H

harbour
a place where ships unload and shelter.

headland
a piece of mainland that juts out into the sea.

hemisphere
relating to the halves of the earth above and below the equator.

horticulture
growing of flowers, fruits and vegetables, and plants for human use.

hydroelectric power
electricity created using the power of water.

I

igneous
a type of rock formed by cooled liquid magma.

industry
a type of work that many people are involved in.

L

Laima Clock
a famous monument and popular meeting point in Riga, Latvia.

landlocked
relating to a country that is surrounded entirely by land.

latitude
how far from the equator a place is.

Latvian
relating to a person, language or object from the country of Latvia.

M

mainland
the main part of a country.

mantle
a layer in the Earth between the core and the crust.

metamorphic
a type of rock formed when heat and pressure are applied to igneous rocks or sedimentary rocks.

meteorologist
a person whose job it is to study the weather.

migrants
people who move or migrate to another country.

motorways
wide roads with many lanes for fast travel used by lots of vehicles.

motto
a short saying or phrase to describe the intention of a group or organisation.

mountain ranges
a group of mountains.

N

native
belonging to a particular place.

O

orbits
move around something, for example the Earth's movement around the sun.

P

Pangaea
a huge continent that existed at a time when Earth's continents were connected to one another.

passing trade
relating to people who make an unplanned stop at a business, such as a shop or restaurant, because they happen to be passing through the area where it is located.

pastime
hobby.

plates
several rigid parts of the Earth's crust which make up its surface.

pollution
contamination of the natural environment by harmful substances released through human activity.

potholing
the exploration of caves deep underground.

provinces
areas of a country with a number of counties.

Q

Quality Bus Corridors
relating to dedicated road space and traffic signal priority being given to buses in Dublin.

R

rain gauge
an instrument used to measure precipitation.

reefs
lines of rocks close to the surface of the sea.

reproduce
to give birth to offspring or young.

river settlements
areas located by a river.

rotation
relating to circular movement on an axis.

S

scenic
relating to a place with beautiful or attractive natural scenery.

sedimentary
relating to a type of rock formed when igneous rocks are broken down, layered upon one another and gradually joined with animal and plant remains over millions of years.

solar system
the sun and the planets that revolve around it.

soot
black powdery substance left from smoke.

spawn
to lay eggs, usually relating to fish like salmon.

species
a group of living things that are very similar to one another.

sunburn
sore redness of the skin caused by sun exposure.

sundial
an instrument that determines the time of day using the position of the sun.

sunstroke
a serious illness caused by over-exposure to the sun.

sustainable
relating to something that can be maintained.

T

thermometer
an instrument for measuring temperature.

tidal energy
power produced by a surge of ocean water.

tour bus
a bus that takes tourists on guided trips around an area.

tundra
relating to a climate zone that is very cold all year.

U

upstream
relating to the journey taken by a salmon back to the stream where it was born.

Ireland

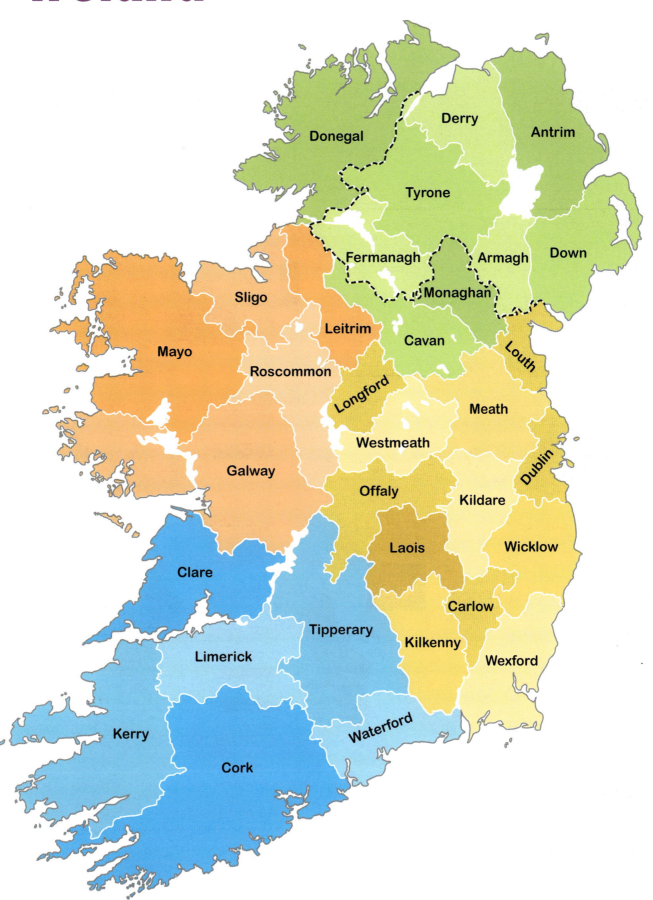

European Union

World Map

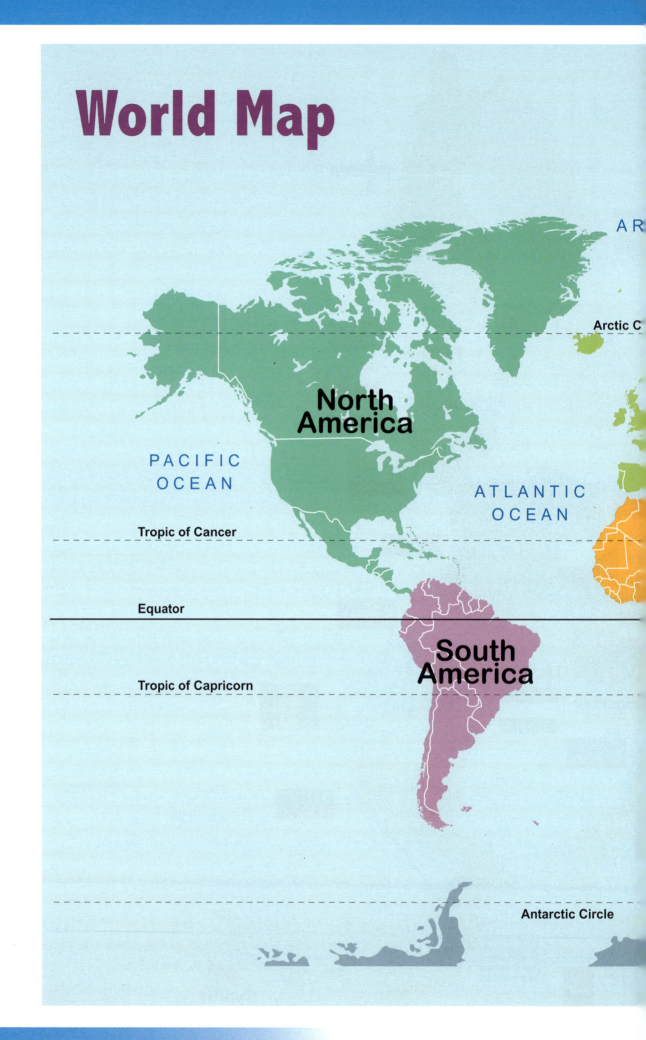

116 Unlocking Geography • 5th Class

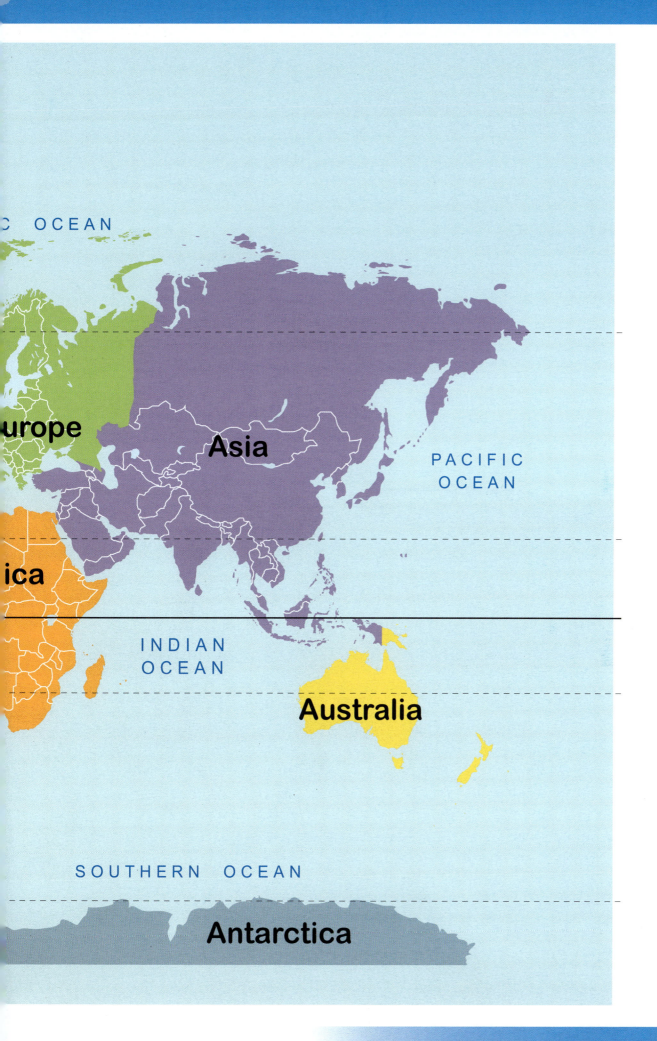